Orkneys

SCOTLAND

① ②
③

①

③
④
⑤
②

IRELAND

①
②
③
⑥

④
⑤

⑥

WALES

ENGLAND

NORTH SEA

⑦ ⑧ ⑨
⑩ ⑪
① ② ⑯
⑫ ⑬
⑰ ⑭
⑮
⑲
⑳ ⑱ ㉓
㉕ ㉔
㉒㉖ ㉙
㉑ ㉗ ㉘ ㉚
㉒ ㉛
㉜

STRAITS OF DOVER

①

FRANCE

First published 1972
Third reprint 1977
Macdonald Educational Ltd
Holywell House, Worship Street
London EC2A 2EN
© Macdonald Educational
Limited 1972

Made and printed by
Hazell Watson & Viney Ltd
Aylesbury
Bucks

Edited by Bridget Hadaway
and Sue Jacquemier
Cover designed by Robert Jackson

ISBN 0 356 03959 5
Library of Congress Catalog Card
No. 72-172430

Cover: *(L)* Daniel Myten's portrait of Sir Thomas Meautys, a wealthy member of the gentry in the seventeenth century. *(TC)* Portrait of an unknown lady, by Nicholas Hilliard. *(BC)* Fountains Abbey, Yorkshire. *(TR)* Engraving of William Shakespeare from the printed First Folio of his plays. *(BR)* The Indian village of Pomeiooc, enclosed by a palisade, painted about 1585.

Title page (opposite): *(L)* A Presbyterian. *(TR)* Charles II on an English Delftware plate of the 1660's. *(BR)* The Tower of London in 1615, depicted by a Dutch traveller.

We wish to thank the following individuals and organisations for their assistance and for making available material in their collections.

Key to picture positions:
(T) top *(C)* centre
(L) left *(B)* bottom *(R)* right
and combinations; for example,
(TC) top centre

Abby Aldrich Rockefeller Folk Art Collection, Virginia *page 63(B)*
Ashmolean Museum, Oxford *page 51(TR)*
Armouries, Tower of London *page 11(BL)*
Batchelor, John *pages 4–5*
Bath, The Marquess of *page 29(T)*
Bedford, His Grace the Duke of *page 33(B)*
Bettman Archive *page 36(R)*
Biblioteca Querini, Stampalia, Venice *page 62*
Bibliothèque Municipale, Cambrai *page 67(TL)*
Bodleian Library *page 13(B)*
British Museum, by courtesy of the Trustees *cover(BR), title page(L), pages 7(BR), 10(L)(R), 14(R), 15(B), 22, 23(BL), 26(R), 27(BR), 30, 32(TR)(BL), 34(TR), 37(T), 47(BL)(BR), 53(TL), 63(TL)(TR), 68(R), 70–71(B)*
Clayton, Peter *pages 19(T), 84(L)*
Cooper, A. C. *cover(L), pages 70(TL), 81(T)*
Courtauld Institute *pages 29(T), 42(R)*
Crown Copyright *cover(BC), pages 11(TL)(TR), 15(TL)(TR), 37(BL), 47(TL), 53(L)*
Culver Pictures Inc. *pages 58(L), 60(L)*
Dean and Chapter of Westminster Abbey *page 8*
de L'Isle, Viscount *pages 24(BL), 31(B)*
Devonshire Chatsworth Collection, reproduced by permission of the Trustees of the Chatsworth Settlement *page 42(C)*

Dixon, C. M. *pages 49(TL), 68(L)*
Drury, Geoffrey *title page (TR), pages 70–71(B)*
Edinburgh University Library *title page(BR), pages 31(T), 43(TL), 64(TL)(BL), 82–83(BL)(BR)*
Editions R. Laffont *pages 54–55*
Edwards, B. J. N. *page 24(TL)*
Exeter College, Oxford *page 45(BC)*
Fitzherbert *page 16(L)*
Fleming, R. B. *pages 15(B), 37(T)*
Folger Shakespeare Library *page 21(BL)*
Frans Halsmuseum, Haarlem *page 57(B)*
Freeman, John *pages 39(T), 49(B)*
Gerson, Mark *pages 16(L), 25(L), 27(BL)*
Giraudon *pages 13(TR), 16(L), 17(B)*
H.M. Queen Elizabeth II, by gracious permission of *page 79(R)*
Hulton Picture Library *cover(TR), pages 13(TL), 17(TR), 23(T)(BR), 25(R), 27(T), 28(L), 29(B), 42(L), 43(TR), 48(R), 50(R), 52, 64(R), 66(R), 67(BR), 69(T), 72(C), 73(B), 74(C), 76(L)(R), 77(B), 78(L), 80(L), 84(R)*
Lennoxlove *page 40(R)*
Lincoln's Inn Library *page 44*
London Museum, by courtesy of the Trustees *page 70(TR)*
Mansell Collection *pages 4(C), 12(C)(R), 17(TL), 20(R), 28(R), 33(TL)(TR), 36(L), 38(L), 41(B), 43(BR), 45(TL)(BL), 46, 50(L), 53(BL), 55(TR), 56, 61(TL)(B), 65(BL), 66(L), 67(BR), 69(B), 72(R), 74(R), 75(B), 78(R), 83(BC), 84(C), 85(BL)(BR)*
Mary Evans Picture Library *pages 43(BL), 47(TR), 58(L), 74(L), 83(T)*
Master and Fellows of Magdalene College, Cambridge *page 32(TL)*
Metropolitan Museum of Art: gift of J. Pierpont Morgan *page 41(TR)*
Musées Royaux des Beaux Arts, Belgium *page 65(R)*
Museo del Prado, Madrid *page 20(L)*
National Gallery of Ireland *pages 34(BL), 38(R), 77(T)*
National Library of Scotland *page 41(TL)*

National Maritime Museum *page 75(T)*
National Portrait Gallery *pages 21(BR), 45(R), 57(T), 72(L)*
Northampton Record Society: the Grafton Collection *page 60(R)*
Palazzo Ducale, Rome *page 7(TL)*
PDAI *pages 19(B), 39(BL)(BR)*
Pierpont Morgan Library *page 80(R)*
Public Record Office, Lancashire *page 24(TL)*
Rees, Alan *pages 19(B), 39(BL)(BR)*
RIBA: drawings collection *page 42(R)*
RIBA Library *page 71(T)*
Ridley, Christopher *pages 8(L), 21(T), 24(BL)*
Robertson *page 39(BL)(BR)*
Scala *page 62*
Science Museum, London *pages 7, 37(BL)*
Scot, Reginald *page 27(BL)*
Scottish National Portrait Gallery *page 40(L)*
Scottish National Portrait Gallery: on loan from the Collection of Lord Primrose *page 51(B)*
Smith, Edwin *page 24(TR)*
Smith, J. C. *page 16(C)*
Society of Apothecaries *page 2*
Speaker, The Rt Hon. Mr, House of Commons *page 47(TL)*
Staatsbibliothek, Berlin *page 65(TL)*
Tate Gallery *pages 26(BL), 70(TL)*
Transglobe *page 40(R)*
University and State Library, Berne *page 12(L)*
Verulam, The Earl of: the Gorhambury Collection *cover(L)*
The Vicar, Church of St Chad *page 49(TL)*
Victoria and Albert Museum *cover(TC), title page(TR), pages 18, 26(TL), 51(TL), 68(L), 79(L), 81(T), 85(TL)*
Viollet, Roger *page 7(TR)*
Westminster Cathedral Library *page 21(TL)*
Dr Williams Library *page 48(L), 49(TR)*
Woodmansterne Limited: Nicholas Servian *page 11(BL)*

Macdonald
Educational

R J Unstead

Struggle for Power

A Pictorial History 1485-1689

Presbyterian

Volume Four

In this book, which covers the period between Henry VII's accession and James II's downfall, the great issue is the struggle for power between King and Parliament. Was the country to be ruled by an absolute monarch, by an assembly of lords, country gentlemen, lawyers and merchants or by a King who observed the laws and heeded the wishes of Parliament?

A civil war and the King's execution provided an answer that turned out to be little to the people's liking and, for a time, they seemed to have exchanged one form of tyranny for another. But, banishing another King in the process, they reached a compromise which developed into their system of government, whereby the King reigns and Parliament rules.

History has to do with many things besides politics, and this period includes another struggle, even more embittered and less capable of a tolerant solution—that between the Catholic and Protestant faiths. We shall look, too, at everyday life, at art, industry and science, at Scottish and Irish affairs, at books and newspapers, at wars, and at the growth of an English-speaking nation in North America.

942

R J Unstead

Struggle for Power

On the left, England's moment of peril—Spanish and English warships engage each other as the Armada pursues its majestic way up-Channel.

Much more than the fate of England hung on the outcome of this sea-battle. If Philip had been victorious, the history of western Europe would have been altered; besides England, the Netherlands must have gone under and France, too, might have succumbed. The Protestants could have been crushed out of existence and a great part of Europe united by force under a common religion and one all-powerful ruler.

In the event, through luck on one side and mismanagement on the other, the Armada was a gigantic failure; its defeat gave the English a legend and a new self-confidence, while demonstrating that Spain had passed its peak.

But legends are powerful and long-lasting. The English people's memory of the Armada helped them to defy both Napoleon and Hitler.

Contents

The New World of America

From ancient times, traders from the East had carried spices, silks and precious goods to Europe's edge; the overland caravan routes were well-established and travellers like Marco Polo brought back tales of fabulous kingdoms and limitless wealth. But this Eastern trade was perilously uncertain. Ferocious tribesmen robbed the caravans, Mongol warriors swept across Asia into eastern Europe and, in 1453, Constantinople itself fell to the Ottoman Turks. The land-route to the East was closed and the wealth of Genoa and Venice seemed certain to shrivel away.

Navigators and geographers began to search for a sea-route to the Indies and some found employment in Portugal where Prince Henry the Navigator was encouraging his sailors to explore the coast of Africa, seeking gold and slaves.

Meanwhile, a Genoese sailor named Columbus put forward a plan to reach Asia by sailing westward across the Atlantic, but he had to plead for years until he found a monarch willing to finance his immortal voyage. He sailed in 1492 and discovered, not a route to the East, but a new continent.

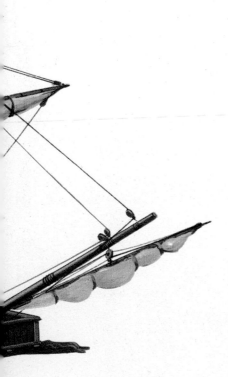

The man who re-discovered America

Born in 1451 in Genoa, Christopher Columbus went to sea as a boy of fourteen and made several voyages which probably included visits to England and Iceland.

Through studying astronomy and perhaps remembering tales of the Norse voyagers from Iceland, he came to the conclusion that the world was round and he could therefore reach Asia by sailing west.

Needing a royal patron, he went to Spain, where, after seven frustrating years, he persuaded King Ferdinand to supply him with three ships.

Columbus's expeditions

On 3rd August 1492, he set sail in the "Santa Maria" and, having reached the Canary Islands, continued west until, on 12th October, an island was sighted which he named San Salvador. After discovering Cuba and Haiti, he returned to Spain.

Christopher Columbus, who unwittingly discovered a continent.

The next year, Columbus discovered more islands but, though a third voyage brought him to the mainland of South America, he quarrelled with the governor and came home in irons.

During his fourth voyage, he explored the Gulf of Mexico and he died in 1506, still believing in the existence of a passage to India.

The flagship of Columbus (left), the *Santa Maria*. 1: The Great Cabin, occupied by Columbus; 2: ports for cannons; 3: after hatch, used by crew; 4: tiller; 5: main hatch; 6: ship's boat.
The *Santa Maria* was about 95 feet long and 25 feet in the beam—no bigger than a modern fishing trawler —with three masts carrying mainsail and topsail, foresail (with another fitted to the bowsprit) and a triangular sail known as the lateen. She carried a crew of 52. The other ships, the *Pinta* and the *Nina* were even smaller, with crews of 18 men.

They reached the West Indies in 69 days but the *Santa Maria* was wrecked off Santo Domingo, so Columbus sailed back to Spain in the *Nina*, taking gold, spices, birds, animals and 10 Indians as proof of his success.

The Round Earth

While the Spaniards and the Portuguese were exploring the coasts of America and venturing to the East, British seamen were still engaged in cross-Channel trade and fishing. But, by Henry VII's reign, the merchants of Bristol were beginning to trade with Spain and to look westward, so they supported the voyages of John Cabot, a Venetian navigator living in the city, when, only five years after Columbus, he sailed to America and discovered Newfoundland.

His failure to find a route to China brought disappointment, but a merchant named William Hawkins began trading along the African coast and Richard Chancellor's expedition, in search of a north-eastern passage to India, ended up in Russia.

In Elizabeth's reign, John Hawkins started the slave trade with Spanish possessions in America. It was his kinsman, Francis Drake, who after some piratical ventures, sailed round the world, robbing Spaniards on their private waters. He claimed California for the Queen and, by his example, convinced Englishmen that they, too, had the audacity and skill to sail the oceans of the world.

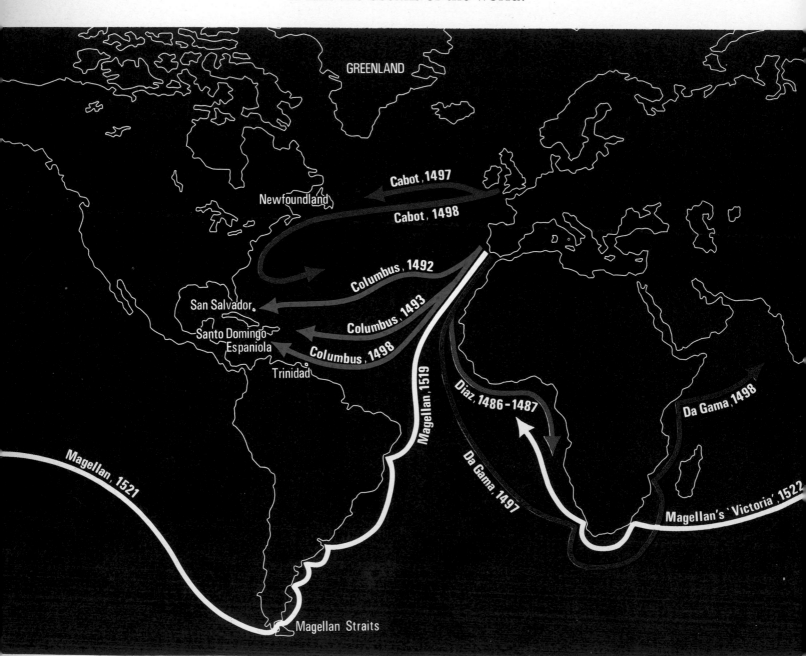

The Cabots

The Cabots: an Italian painting showing John and Sebastian Cabot, with the lands they were said to have discovered. John, or Giovanni, a citizen of Venice, who had settled in Bristol, made two voyages to America but we are less sure of Sebastian's exploits.

Impressed by the foreign navigator's claim that he could reach the East by sailing west, Henry VII gave Giovanni Caboto (John Cabot) leave to prepare an expedition. Cabot sailed in 1497 and explored the coasts of Newfoundland and Labrador, without finding anything more valuable than codfish. A second voyage was no more successful.

His son Sebastian posed as a maritime expert but, finding no support from Henry VIII, went to Spain and became Pilot-Major.

After a disastrous failure in South America, he returned to England and was later appointed "chief setter-forth" of the voyage which took Richard Chancellor to Russia.

Sebastian Cabot (1457–1537), mapmaker and "Pilot-Major of Spain".

The great explorers

The map on the left shows the routes taken by five explorers who in the space of barely thirty years solved problems which had baffled men for centuries. Not only did they prove that the world was round, but they discovered a continent whose existence had been unsuspected by anyone except perhaps the Vikings.

The first of the voyages was that of Bartholomew Diaz who, in 1487, set out from Portugal and sailed down the coast of Africa as far as the Cape of Good Hope. Next, came Columbus's voyages to the New World; these added to man's knowledge but, like Cabot's voyages from England, proved disappointing to those who longed for the riches of the East. Meanwhile, the Portuguese redoubled their efforts and Vasco da Gama, taking a great curved route to the Cape, sailed on to India and set up trade relations with the princes.

Magellan's incredible voyage

Then occurred the greatest voyage in history. In 1519, Ferdinand Magellan, a Portuguese captain in the service of Spain, set out for America, rounded its southern cape, entered the Pacific Ocean and, after appalling hardships and near-starvation, reached the Spice Islands. Magellan himself was killed but eighteen survivors of his crew brought their battered vessel back to Seville. They were the first men to sail round the world.

Map of the Americas from the atlas of Gerard Mercator of Flanders who, in 1559, produced a method of mapmaking which is still used.

The New World

Columbus believed that he had reached the Orient but it was not long before nothing remained of his claim, apart from calling his islands "the West Indies". It was clear that a huge land-mass lay between Europe and Asia by the western route.

The first maps of the New World were made by Juan de la Costa, who sailed with Columbus; he recorded the Caribbean Islands, over 1000 miles of North American coast charted by the Cabots, and Brazil.

Unknown continents

Magellan's voyage showed the extent of South America, the existence of the Pacific and the fact that the New World consisted of two land-masses joined by a slender isthmus. Early maps included a vast unknown continent in the south, *Terra Australis Incognita*.

7

The Beginning of Modern England

After thirty years of strife, the house of Lancaster triumphed on Bosworth Field and, although the Yorkists made only futile attempts to regain the English throne, Henry Tudor was astute enough to make the kingdom safe for his son. By marrying Elizabeth of York, Edward IV's daughter, he intended to put an end to the long-standing feud.

Next, he dealt with the nobles. Too weakened to resist strong measures, they had to bow to his orders to disband their armies of retainers and to look on helplessly while he appointed men of his own choosing to run the kingdom's business. Above all else, Henry VII realised that money was power, and he raked it in by every possible means; but he also created wealth by encouraging trade.

Having outwitted his enemies at home, he made England respected abroad through treaties, alliances and royal marriages. At his death, Henry left his son a prosperous, confident country, with good government, obedient nobles and a full Treasury—a small kingdom but one that was ready to play a part in a world that had suddenly become much wider.

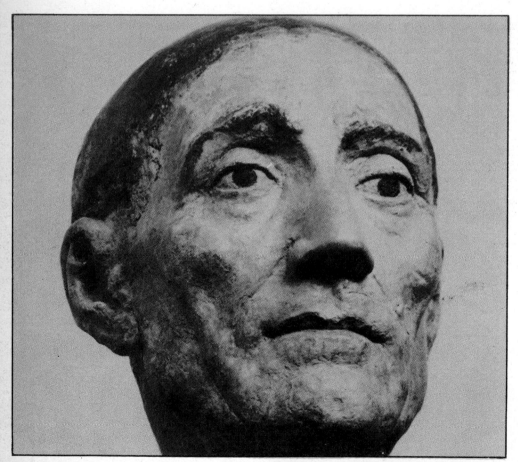

Death-mask of Henry VII: his care-worn face expresses his power to weigh up men and situations.

Henry VII's reign

Almost at once, Henry had to cope with Yorkist plots and rebellious Cornishmen. Two imposters came forward—Lambert Simnel claiming to be Edward IV's nephew, and Perkin Warbeck who declared himself to be the younger prince from the Tower. Both imposters were unmasked and every dangerous Yorkist put out of harm's way.

Meanwhile, Henry amassed money by fines, "benevolences" and a large gift from the King of France to go home without fighting. Spain's friendship was won by the marriage of Henry's son to Catherine of Aragon, and Scotland was appeased by his daughter's marriage to James IV.

An official guide to weights and measures

On the right is a chart of weights and measures issued in Henry VII's reign as the official guide to market supervisors. It was evidently a ready-reckoner to enable the "clerk of the market" to settle disputes by looking up the standard measures and by pointing to the impressive pictures of the King and his judges, as well as to the dishonest stall-holder with his head in the pillory.

Pottells and hogsheads

On the chart, we can find such long-forgotten measures as "Two grains (of wheat) maketh ye 16th part of a penny"; actual weight of money was clearly important, because (top right) "Two pence halfpenny the 8th part of an ounce" and so on. There are clear illustrations of hogsheads, tuns and elegant wine jugs, informing us that "Two quarts maketh one pottell" and "Two pottells maketh a gallon for wine and ale". Finally, at the bottom, right, we learn that "twenty hundred weight maketh a Tonne" and, in case land measurement was needed, "40 rods in length and 4 of breadth maketh an acre" (i.e. 220 yards by 22 yards).

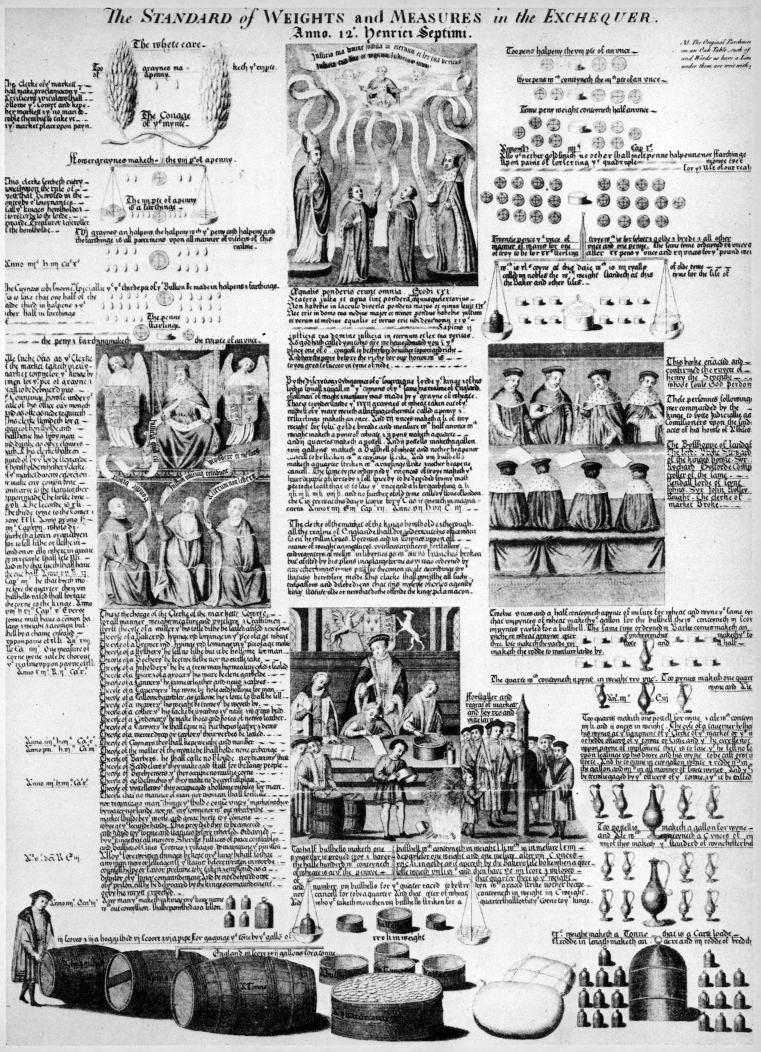

Tudor Armies and Defences

In the fourteenth century, the English had been the finest soldiers in Europe but, by the end of the Wars of the Roses, their armies had become old-fashioned. New fighting methods had developed on the Continent, where professional armies consisted of massed columns of Swiss and German pikemen, supported by companies armed with hand-guns, instead of cross-bows. Heavy cavalry had come back into its own, with horses as fully armoured as their riders. A variety of cannons accompanied the armies for use in battles and at sieges.

By contrast, the English were ill-equipped. Henry VII's ban on "Livery and Maintenance" (the keeping of uniformed troops) had put an end to private armies, so that, at his accession, Henry VIII had no standing army, apart from the Yeomen of the Guard. The militia still existed in theory, though its weapons consisted mainly of poleaxes and longbows, and there was a general shortage of cavalry horses, armour and guns. Henry therefore applied himself to building up a stock of modern weapons, while looking to the kingdom's defences against invasion.

One of Henry VIII's soldiers, almost certainly a Spaniard, or an Italian mercenary. He wears a sword and a powder-flask, and carries a matchlock or handgun; in his hand, he holds the slow-match, a slow-burning cord soaked in saltpetre and dried. Held by the curved lever ("serpentine") you can see on his gun, the cord's lighted end was pushed into the touch-hole by pressing the rear lever beneath the stock of the gun.

A Royal Guard of Henry VIII's household:
Henry added to the Yeomen of the Guard, a second body called "the King's Spears", who consisted of gentlemen in armour, each accompanied by a mounted archer, a horseman and a servant. Known later as the Gentlemen-at-Arms, they carried a mace when on palace duty and this became a symbol of authority, as can still be seen in law-courts and in the Houses of Parliament.

Left: St Mawes Castle, Cornwall, built by van Haschenperg, a German "deviser", for Henry VIII, to defend the anchorage at Falmouth as part of his system of coastal defence.

Above: an aerial view of Walmer Castle, Kent, an artillery fort, built in 1539 to defend the Downs (an anchorage) against French attack. Walmer, Deal and Sandown castles stood on the coast, one mile from each other.

Henry VIII's armaments

To strengthen the kingdom's defences and, if the opportunity arose, to win military glory, Henry VIII undertook an energetic policy of rearmament.

Firstly, he built naval dockyards at Deptford and Woolwich and kept up a permanent navy; secondly, he fortified the coast by building a new type of castle like the ones above; thirdly, he amassed arms and made weapon practice and archery compulsory for all able-bodied men; fourthly, he set up gun-foundries and, fifthly, he established a royal armour factory.

Armour and cannon

To start with, he had to buy several thousand suits of armour from the Continent, but to avoid being dependent on foreign suppliers, he brought over groups of armourers from Brussels, Italy and Germany to work for him at Greenwich.

As regards guns, he began in the same way by buying cannon from Hans Poppenruyter, a famous gunfounder of Flanders, but soon he was employing the Arcanus brothers from Italy and Peter Baude of France to run his own foundries at Houndsditch and Salisbury Place. At his death, Henry possessed 64 brass guns and 351 made of iron.

A suit of armour of Henry VIII of about 1514, made for combat on foot in tournaments. The collar flange was designed to guard against an upward slash.

11

The Church is Split

The Reformation—that is, the break-away from the Church of Rome—began as a movement of protest. The medieval Church's power and wealth, its perpetual demands for money, and the sins and omissions of the clergy caused widespread indignation that had long been expressed by men like John Wyclif and John Huss of Bohemia. In Germany, a friar named Martin Luther attacked the Pope so venomously and won such support that a separate Church was established.

In England, however, Luther's teachings made little headway and Henry VIII was rewarded by the Pope for writing a book against Luther. The break with Rome came through a personal matter. After eighteen years of marriage to Catherine of Aragon, Henry had no son; so, on the grounds of having married his brother's widow, he asked the Pope to annul the marriage. The Pope, virtually a prisoner of Catherine's nephew, could not oblige Henry and, after a remarkable display of patience, Henry decided to renounce the Pope's authority, to make himself Head of the Church and to marry the woman who might provide him with a son and heir.

A satire on greedy monks: this 16th century woodcut shows a monk with the head of a wolf who has seized an innocent lamb.

The Reformation in Europe

Criticism of the Church began in Italy in the fourteenth century when Marsilius of Padua declared that priests ought to give up their wealth and worldly powers.

John Huss of Bohemia, a follower of Wyclif, went to the stake in 1415 for continuing the attacks. His ideas spread to Germany, where Luther became the fiery champion of the "new religion", which rejected the Pope and advocated a simpler faith, without saints, monasteries and unmarried priests.

Other leaders came to the fore, such as Zwingli of Switzerland, Bucer in Germany and the Frenchman, John Calvin of Geneva, who preached a religion without priests but with a strict, even harsh, way of life. The Lutheran and the Calvinist Churches emerged, while in France, Protestants became known as Huguenots.

Henry VIII and Archbishop Cranmer trampling the Pope's authority underfoot; in the background, *Religion* replaces decaying *Superstition*.

The Reformation in England

Though he renounced the Pope, destroyed the monasteries and set himself up as Head of the English Church, Henry VIII was no Protestant and, to the end of his life, he persecuted Protestant leaders.

Though he allowed Cranmer to have his English Bible read in church, he remained a Catholic at heart and it was not until after his death that the Latin Mass was

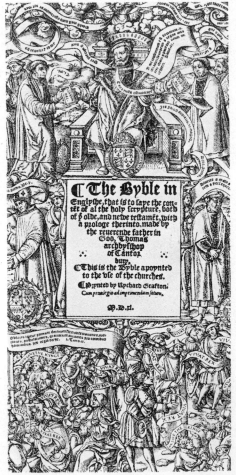

Title page of Cranmer's Bible of 1539, written in English.

replaced by Cranmer's Prayer Book and extreme steps were taken to abolish ceremony and to destroy sacred pictures and images.

Catherine of Aragon, Henry VIII's devoted wife, whose only fault was her failure to bear a son. A popular Queen, she was a lively, capable woman whom Henry genuinely loved.

Anne Boleyn, the second wife, whom nobody liked, except King Henry.

No heir to the throne

Contrary to popular belief, Henry VIII was a model husband to his first wife. He loved his Spanish bride and, as far as we know, had no affairs after he married her.

Catherine was not barren, for she produced several children but, owing perhaps to poor medical knowledge or to a disease, all but one died. Two were still-born, one lived for a few hours and the much-desired son survived for two months. Only Princess Mary lived to become Queen of England.

Poor Catherine's last pregnancy was in 1518, when she was thirty-three, but it was not until 1527 that Henry voiced his opinion that their marriage had not been blessed by God because he had married his brother's widow and that, according to the Old Testament, was a sin.

Part of Catherine's pathetic but dignified letter to her husband.

The six wives of Henry VIII

In 1533, after Cranmer had declared Henry's marriage to **Catherine of Aragon** to be illegal, the King married **Anne Boleyn**. Their first child was Elizabeth; later, two boys were born dead.

Perhaps Henry then grew tired of Anne, for she was suddenly charged with infidelity and beheaded. Almost at once, Henry married **Jane Seymour** who, in 1537, produced the longed-for son and died.

For two years, the grief-stricken husband remained single, before yielding to his minister Cromwell's persuasion to marry a German bride, **Anne of Cleves**.

She was speedily banished with a pension and the ageing monarch next married **Catherine Howard**, whose youthful love affairs, when they came to light, caused her to be sent to the executioner's block.

The sixth and last wife was **Catherine Parr**, a discreet widow who managed to outlive the old tyrant.

A Prince of the Renaissance

The Renaissance—the revival of the learning and art of the Greeks and Romans—began in Italy and came late to England. The Italian city-states, Florence in particular, were ideally suited to studying the ancients and to developing new ways of thinking and new forms of art, for the cities and their universities were free from close control by kings and priests. The citizens governed themselves; merchants and princelings became patrons of learning and art. So, from about 1300, Italy produced artists like Giotto, Leonardo da Vinci and Michelangelo, poets and writers like Petrarch, Boccaccio, Macchiavelli and Dante, and patrons like Lorenzo the Magnificent whose court was the home of artists and scholars.

This brilliant outburst of creative energy spread north, where Erasmus was the greatest of the Humanists, as these new scholars were called, and it came to England which, owing to geography and internal wars, had to some extent remained cut off from these exciting developments. Henry VIII—rich, a gifted athlete, poet and musician—was, in his own opinion and in the eyes of the world, a prince of the Renaissance.

The new learning in England

One of the first patrons of the new learning in England was Humphrey, Duke of Gloucester, who, in Henry VI's boyhood, made himself the friend of scholars and collected the finest library in the country.

Henry VI loved beautiful things and built the magnificent chapel at King's College, Cambridge, though civil war and shortage of money put an end to these civilised interests.

However, the tide turned when Edward IV gained the throne, for he encouraged Caxton's printing enterprise and built the superb St George's Chapel at Windsor. Even the miser-king, Henry VII, allowed himself to be persuaded by his cultured mother, Lady Margaret Beaufort, to find money for the arts and to employ William Vertue to design his chapel at Westminster.

One factor in the spread of Renaissance culture was the surprisingly large numbers of foreigners living in England—Italians, Flemings, Germans—who undertook artistic commissions and also worked as scribes, copying classical and French manuscripts.

Scholars of the Renaissance

The Renaissance was not confined to the visual arts of painting, sculpture and architecture; the Dutchman, Erasmus, a great classical scholar who realised how the new printing-presses could help to spread learning, was often in England. He was the friend of John Colet, Dean

Henry VIII playing on a harp: he was also proficient on the lute and, like most educated people of his time, he could read music at sight. He composed several pieces of music but none seems to have survived, though some people believe that he wrote the well-known tune *Greensleeves*.

While English painting and sculpture could not rival the work of the Italian masters, the English were looked upon as the most musical nation in Europe. At Court and in family circles, they astonished foreigners by their skill and enjoyment in playing and singing.

Henry passed on his musical talent to his daughters Mary and Elizabeth.

of St Paul's, John Fisher and Thomas More, scholars and humanists who were deeply concerned with religion and the abuses of the Church. Men like these founded schools and wrote copiously on the ways to educate the young.

A gifted King

Henry VIII became heir to this passion for learning. His father and his learned grandmother, Margaret, saw that he was well-grounded in religious studies, history and music; he knew Latin, French, Spanish and Italian; his tutor, Skelton, was a poet. More and Erasmus came to see him and the gifted boy grew up able to play several instruments, to compose music and poetry, to write fluently and to excel in mathematics.

Fountains Abbey, in Yorkshire, the great Cistercian monastery closed down on Henry VIII's orders in 1536.

Ruins of Whitby Abbey, a Benedictine monastery and one of the oldest in England.

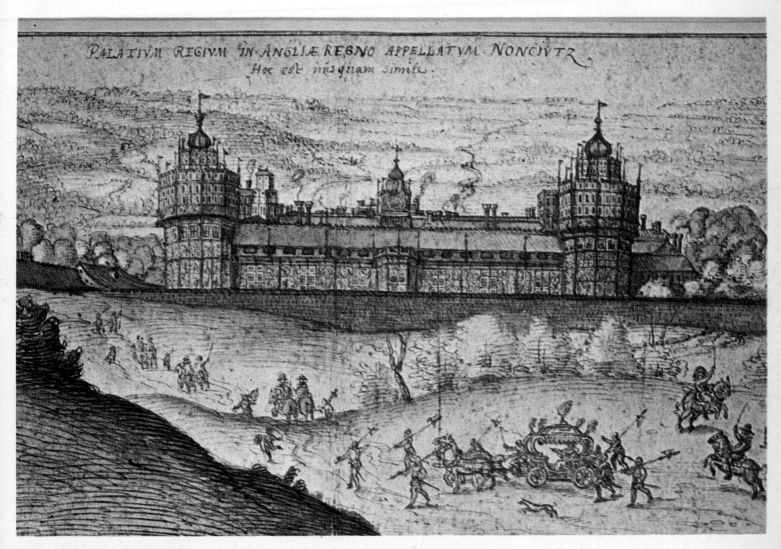

PALATIVM REGIVM IN ANGLIÆ REGNO APPELLATVM NONCIVTZ. Hoc est nisquam simile.

Nonsuch Palace, Henry VIII's tremendous residence which was more in the Renaissance style than Wolsey's masterpiece, Hampton Court, 6 miles away. English, Dutch, French and Italian artists decorated the palace and laid out its grounds. It was one of Elizabeth I's favourite palaces.

Dissolution of the monasteries

In 1536, Henry's Minister, Thomas Cromwell, closed 400 of the smaller monasteries and, in the next four years, dissolved the remainder of the religious houses. Nearly all the monks and nuns received pensions but the monastic plate, jewellery and money went straight into Henry's Treasury.

The monastic libraries were mostly lost or wantonly destroyed.

Mastering a Trade

The Tudor age saw some remarkable industrial progress and some new industrial problems. Tyneside was by far the most important coal-producing area in England and its output was in high demand by the brewers, salt-makers, glass-manufacturers and soap-makers. Coal was also becoming commonly used by housewives, now that people were adding chimneys to their houses and wood was becoming increasingly scarce. But coal was less suitable for iron-smelting than charcoal and with the ship-builders also needing timber, there was great concern about the country's dwindling forests.

These industrial developments called for large amounts of money and for tighter control of workers' hours and wages. Miners in Scotland and the north of England were virtually slaves, but, with a surplus of labour, the workers' bargaining power was low. One of the great problems of Tudor industry was the lack of a good home market; the rich could afford luxury goods, the state bought guns and assisted ship-building, but the common people earned too little to have money to spare for industrial goods.

Ploughing—a woodcut from Fitzherbert's *Husbondrye* of 1525, written to help improve farming.

Woodcarving of a fuller; he cleansed the raw cloth of oil and grease with fuller's earth.

The Craftsman—a skilled joiner uses a plane in his home workshop, while his wife spins.

"Sheep eat men"

In the sixteenth century, population rose faster than food production, thus causing a shortage of land and high prices. The misery of the poor was made worse when landlords enclosed common land in order to keep sheep, depriving the cottager of his right to graze a cow. They also "engrossed" land, i.e. put two or three farms together, employing fewer labourers.

The workers

Though large-scale industry had its beginnings in Tudor times, the typical worker toiled at home in his cottage, in a small workshop with three or four others or as apprentice, labourer or master in a one-man business.

None of the new industries could rival the woollen cloth industry, which produced the most valuable export. Apart from cloth, home industries included building, joinery, leathercrafts, brewing and glass-making, but England was not yet an industrial nation and needed German miners, Flemish weavers and French glass-workers to teach new skills.

High quality and luxury goods, such as silks, furs and exquisite silverware had to be imported, as well as tallow, tar, rope and tall masts for the ship-building industry.

Iron-smelting

The major breakthrough in the iron industry was the development of the blast-furnace, which could produce 100 to 500 tons of cast iron in a year.

Henry VIII's urgent need for the home production of cannons caused the forested Weald (in Kent and Sussex) to become the major iron-producing centre, with 49 blast furnaces out of a total of 85 in the country by the year 1600. Others were built in Monmouthshire, Glamorganshire and the Forest of Dean where there were still ample supplies of timber to produce the all-important charcoal.

A smelting works, 1556 (left); furnace and bellows in the background; a worker quenches a red-hot ingot.

Brewing beer in the early 16th century (right), an industry that employed more workers than mining.

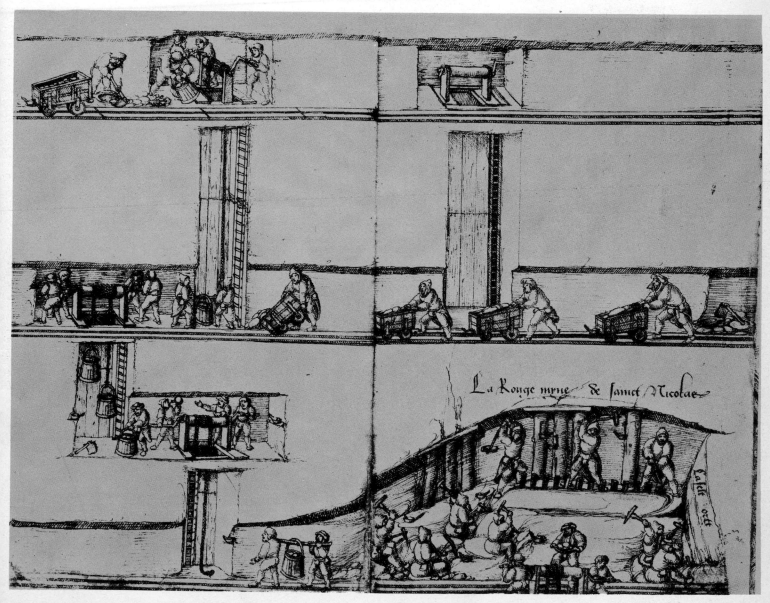

Shafts and underground galleries of a 16th-century French silver-mine. The workings seem more complex than in most English coal-mines of the period, which were simple pits or horizontal tunnels into the hillsides. Coalfields were often owned by the gentry who obtained them cheaply when Church lands were taken over.

The North-East Passage

While the Spaniards and Portuguese were discovering the Americas and a sea-route to India, Englishmen showed little interest in maritime adventures and, after the comparative failure of Cabot's voyages, they allowed fifty years to pass without exerting themselves. But it gradually dawned on them that they were shut out from the fabulous riches of the East.

The Pope had declared that the New World belonged exclusively to Spain and Portugal; German merchants controlled most of the trade of northern Europe and English finances were in a desperate plight. Somehow, a way had to be found to Cathay (China), Cipango (Japan) and the Spice Islands (Indonesia).

In Edward VI's reign, old Sebastian Cabot favoured the idea of reaching China by sailing along the Arctic coasts of Europe and Asia. The North-East Passage, as it was called, would surely lead to the gold and spices of the East. A Merchant Adventurers' Company was formed to equip a fleet of three vessels; under the command of Sir Hugh Willoughby, this little fleet set sail from the Thames in 1553.

"Half-sovereigns" of Edward VI.

The need for trade

By the end of Henry VIII's reign, England was faced with a financial crisis. Wars, huge expenditure on the navy and defence, and the King's extravagance, had brought the country near to bankruptcy.

Moreover, this was a period of inflation, partly because Henry debased the coinage. The amount of pure silver in each coin was much reduced and, while this produced a temporary profit for the King, it caused prices to rocket and hampered trade because no-one knew the true value of money.

Hence, by Edward VI's reign, it was essential to discover new openings for trade; Chancellor's voyage led to the formation of the Muscovy Company and the beginning of England's overseas trade.

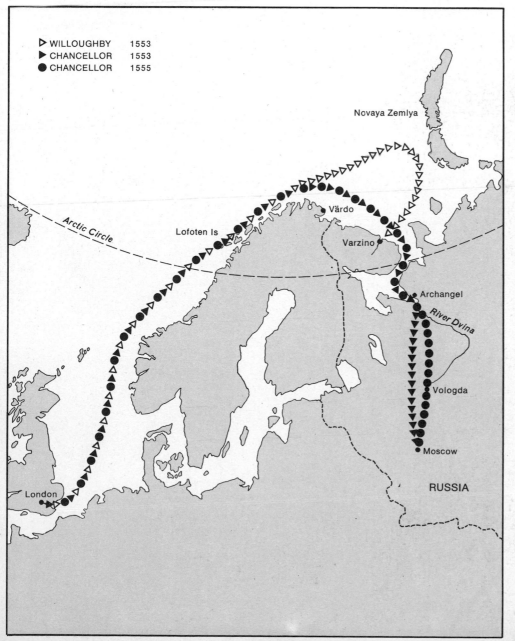

▷ WILLOUGHBY 1553
▶ CHANCELLOR 1553
● CHANCELLOR 1555

Novaya Zemlya

Arctic Circle

Värdo

Lofoten Is

Varzino

Archangel

River Dvina

Vologda

Moscow

London

RUSSIA

An Englishman in Moscow

Sir Hugh Willoughby's Pilot-General was a young Bristol man named Richard Chancellor, whom he put in command of the "Edward Bonaventure". The three ships sailed to the Lofoten Islands, where the captains agreed, in case they were separated, to meet at the harbour of Värdo.

Chancellor battled through a storm and waited for his companions at Värdo, but they never arrived. Blown off course, Willoughby and his crews were frozen to death on a remote northern shore.

Chancellor sailed on into the White Sea and reached the port of Archangel in the almost unknown land of Muscovy, as Russia was called. He made a 1500-mile journey by sledge to Moscow where the Czar, Ivan the Terrible, received him in barbaric splendour and gave him cordial letters to Edward VI. Chancellor returned to England with news that he had opened the way for trade with a new country and, next year, he re-visited Moscow but on the voyage home his ship was wrecked and he perished off the coast of Scotland.

The voyages of Willoughby and Chancellor (left): they established trade in English cloth and Russian furs, hides and tallow.

Russian *boyars* or nobles (far left), whose hats, Chancellor discovered, indicated their rank of nobility, and who lived in mortal dread of the all-powerful Czar, Ivan the Terrible.

Mary Tudor

While, unhappily, there are places where religious intolerance still exists, it is not easy for us to comprehend the cruelty with which sixteenth century people treated one another in the name of religion. The Reformation led to a counter-Reformation, so that a monarch like Philip II of Spain felt it his duty to force Protestants to give up their religion.

In England, where the Duke of Northumberland had Lady Jane Grey proclaimed Queen in an attempt to secure the Protestant succession, Mary Tudor gained her rightful throne. With single-minded zeal, she was determined to bring her people back to the Catholic Church; she therefore married Philip of Spain and re-introduced the laws against heresy.

The first Protestant martyr was burned at Smithfield in 1555 and, in the next three years, nearly 300 others followed him to the stake. But Mary failed. Persecution strengthened the obstinacy of sincere believers, while those who had acquired Church lands were determined to keep them. Mary's policy led only to a deep and lasting hatred of Catholics who, in their turn, were to suffer for religion's sake.

Philip II of Spain (above), husband of Mary Tudor, a dedicated Catholic who devoted his life to ruling his empire and crushing Protestantism.

The fall of Calais, 1558 (right): the English had held the town and a strip of surrounding country for 200 years and regarded it as part of England. The French attacked in such strength that a weak garrison, lacking naval support, was forced to surrender after only 3 days.

The Spanish marriage

The English heartily disliked the marriage of their Queen to Philip II of Spain; their contempt for foreigners was well-known and they resented the idea of England becoming part of the Spanish empire, ruled perhaps like the Netherlands, with Spanish soldiers and the dreaded Inquisition in command.

Sir Thomas Wyatt led a force of Kentishmen to London but the revolt petered out.

Once married to Philip, Mary was bound to involve England in Spanish affairs and was dragged into a war with France that resulted in the loss of Calais, England's last continental possession.

The mystic power of a queen: a 16th century picture shows Mary touching a sick subject to cure the "King's Evil", a tubercular disease called scrofula.

"Bloody Mary"

Despite this title, Mary I was in many ways the gentlest and most likeable of the Tudor monarchs. With her mother, Catherine of Aragon, she suffered neglect and humiliation with noble dignity and her sufferings deepened the intensity of her religious faith, though it does not appear to have occurred to her that persecution might have the same effect on Protestants.

She was not naturally a cruel person, but she believed that it was better for heretics to die than to live in mortal sin. The horror which her persecution implanted in English minds is somewhat curious, for this was a cruel age in which Henry VIII behaved like a savage monster and Elizabeth I, an unusually squeamish monarch, was to execute some 200 Roman Catholics.

By continental standards, the deaths of 300 Protestants was nothing exceptional but, of these, only a handful were well-known persons, such as Hooper, Latimer, Ridley and Cranmer, for most of the leading Protestants had fled abroad; the rest were humble folk—artisans, shop-keepers and the like—whose deaths aroused wider indignation than if they had been nobles.

An unhappy Queen

Yet, it is impossible not to pity Mary. Her whole life was a tragedy and her marriage to Philip brought neither happiness nor the Catholic heir for whom she longed. In the end, ill and deserted by her cold-hearted husband, hated by her subjects whom she had meant to serve so dutifully, she died, crushed by unhappiness and by the final humiliation of losing Calais.

Ye shall be led before Princes and Rulers for my names sake. Matthew 10.

An illustration from Foxe's *Book of Martyrs* (left) showing Protestants arrested during Mary's reign being led, roped together, to stand trial for heresy.

Queen of England for 9 days—Lady Jane Grey (above), cousin to Mary and Elizabeth, was only 16 when she was executed in 1554.

Foxe's "Book of Martyrs"

One reason why the Marian persecution burned so deeply into English minds was the reading of Foxe's "Book of Martyrs" by humble and uneducated folk. Written by John Foxe and published in 1560, it contained stories and pictures of Protestants suffering for their religion. Elizabeth ordered a copy to be placed in every Church.

The story of Lady Jane Grey

When Edward VI's health failed, Northumberland hit on a plan to retain the Protestant succession and his own power as head of state. He married his son to fifteen-year-old Lady Jane Grey, the Protestant great-niece of Henry VIII, and, on Edward's death, had the protesting girl proclaimed Queen of England.

However, the country rallied to Mary, and Northumberland was executed. Jane was imprisoned in the Tower, but Mary had no wish to harm her until it was made clear that she could be a rallying-point for the Protestants.

From that moment, Jane was doomed. Refusing to save herself by adopting the Catholic religion, she went bravely to the scaffold on Tower Green.

The Golden Age of Elizabeth

The death of Mary I brought to the throne her sister, Elizabeth, whose reign was to blossom into England's Golden Age. Yet, at her accession, few would have dared to predict such triumph, for the country was divided over religion, its Treasury was empty, its navy rotten and its forces too weak to withstand the victorious French.

By patience and cunning, Elizabeth survived, fending off her enemies and suitors and making a religious settlement that drove no-one to rebellion. Her people called her "Gloriana", and she became the focal point in their new pride in being Englishmen—a people who had defied the Pope and would still defy all their enemies abroad.

At Court and when she went about the country, Elizabeth was treated with reverence that amounted almost to worship; she attracted gifted men and inspired them to compose music and sonnets, as well as to sail and to fight. With this revival of English spirit and energy came an astonishing flowering of the English language in prose, poetry and, above all, in the plays of Marlowe and Shakespeare.

A book illustration of 1589 shows Elizabeth saluting her people from a triumphal chariot. Each summer, she would set out on a royal "progress" through the more important counties of the kingdom, riding on horseback with an enormous retinue until, nearing a town, she would seat herself in the springless open chariot from which she could see the people and be seen.

After the Mayor and aldermen had presented her with loyal speeches and rich gifts, she would stay several days at the home of some noble lord who often well-nigh ruined himself in order to put on entertainments worthy of the adored Queen.

Music flourished throughout the Tudor period and here you can see some masked musicians playing (left to right) a tenor lute, the virginal (an early form of piano), treble viol and bass viol. Music was composed for entertainments, dances and songs and, despite the Reformation, there was also a great deal of magnificent Church music.

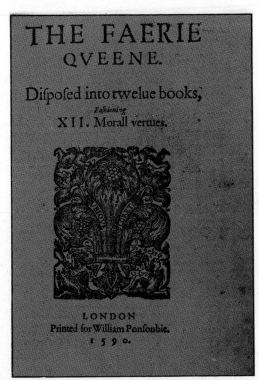

Title page of Edmund Spenser's *The Faerie Queene*. Spenser, son of a tailor, went to grammar school and Cambridge, where he probably began his long poem, *The Shepherd's Calendar*.

After a spell in London, he became secretary to the Lord Deputy of Ireland, where he met Sir Walter Raleigh. On reading *The Faerie Queene*, Raleigh realised that this was a masterpiece far in advance of other English poetry and he had it published and presented to Elizabeth.

The poem tells how the knights of Gloriana undertook adventures in her honour, but it is full of fantasy and marvellous word pictures. Its mastery of language and rhythm influenced later poets.

Thomas Tallis, a notable Elizabethan musician and composer, was the last organist at Waltham Abbey before Henry VIII closed the monastery.

However, the English Reformation did not put an end to choirs and Church music, and Tallis became organist of the Queen's Chapel Royal.

He wrote music which is still sung in English churches and was tutor to William Byrd, the greatest composer of the age, who wrote sacred music, songs and many charming madrigals.

A generation of writers

Even if Shakespeare had never lived, the Elizabethan age would be remarkable for its sudden output of literature. This was the belated English Renaissance, when courtier-soldiers like Raleigh, Surrey and Sir Philip Sidney wrote poems and sonnets of high quality and Edmund Spenser's poetry compared with that of the Italian masters.

Playwrights of the period, including Shakespeare, showed an amazing array of talent; they included Webster, Dekker, Beaumont and Fletcher, Ben Jonson and Christopher Marlowe.

Music and painting

The triumphs of the Elizabethan musicians were less striking, because the English had a long tradition of making and enjoying music at all levels, and, great as were the compositions of Tallis, Byrd and Dowland, they could not compare, at least in quantity, with Italian music.

The same is true of painting and architecture. The Englishman, Nicholas Hilliard, produced some exquisite miniatures, and Tudor houses possessed charm and originality, but in neither case could they equal the masterpieces that were common-place in Italy.

Elizabethans at Home

With civil war ended and the once-mighty nobles poorer and put firmly in their place, Elizabeth's reign saw a boom in house-building. Castles and fortified manors were no longer needed, and the rising class of rich farmers and merchants could afford to build handsome houses in stone, in timber and plaster or in the now-plentiful brick.

The new homes were warmer and more comfortable than any that had so far been built. Glass windows of unprecedented size were set in frames that opened and shut, and every room had its fireplace, so stacks of shapely chimneys became a striking feature of the house. Rooms were panelled in oak, floored with timber or black and white tiles and given Italian-style ceilings of plaster moulded into intricate patterns.

Carpets and rugs began to be placed on the floors instead of rushes; tapestries and velvet hangings were highly prized and, if furniture was solid and none too plentiful, fine linen and glass, plates and vessels of silver and pewter appeared on the dining-table. A garden with geometrical flower-beds completed the setting.

The estate of Lytham Hall, Lancashire, showing the mansion with its tall chimneys, and neighbouring village.

Moreton Hall, Cheshire, a beautifully preserved example of an Elizabethan black-and-white mansion, which owes its striking appearance to the patterning of dark timbers and white plaster.

The Great Hall of Penshurst Place, Sir Philip Sydney's home, which retained in Tudor times this medieval feature of a nobleman's house.

Mansions and houses

The Elizabethan gentleman was usually his own architect, building his house as his fancy took him, yet somehow achieving a style that was attractive and entirely English.

As a rule, he abandoned the medieval plan of building round a courtyard, but erected a long central portion with a porch in the middle and a wing at either end, so the house took the shape of a capital E.

In big mansions, the Great Hall was still needed for banquets and revels, but a new feature was the Long Gallery upstairs, a wide corridor running the length of the house and furnished with fireplaces and window-seats, so the family and their friends could walk up and down, play games, make music and practise swordsmanship.

In addition, there was also a whole range of parlours, bedchambers, offices, dining-rooms and the library. Kitchens, buttery, dairy and still-room (where preserves were made) now came under one roof, instead of being outbuildings.

Smaller houses, two and sometimes three storeys high, were generally built with a framework of oak posts and beams, the spaces between the timbers being filled in with rubble and plastered over.

Door-posts were often carved and the plaster might be shaped into decorated patterns. The timber joists for the second floor were cut somewhat longer than those for the first, so that the second storey jutted out and, in towns, the houses seemed to overhang the streets.

Family life

In Elizabethan homes, the husband was absolute master. His wife obeyed him; his children called him "Sir", doffed their hats in his presence and knelt down to make a request.

If he chose, he was free to beat his wife and, at their marriage, he took possession of her lands and goods. In any case, their marriage was arranged by parents, without regard to their ages or to whether they even knew each other.

A housewife's duties

However, once married, the wife had to run the household and, in large mansions, she needed organising ability of a high order. Her staff of servants had to be set to their daily tasks, from baking bread to brewing ale, while supplies had to be laid in, not for a week, but for months ahead when winter and bad roads would isolate the house.

In addition to the salting of meat and fish, and the making of all kinds of preserves, the housewife would organise the buying of cloth and sewing of clothes; everyday articles, such as soap and candles were made at home, though it was becoming increasingly possible to buy such goods in towns.

Doctor and teacher

The housewife's duties did not end in the kitchen. She was expected to be skilled in making medicines and ointments from herbs and wild plants, for coughs and stomach disorders were everyday ailments.

Each year, she had a baby but most died in infancy, and the children who survived were strictly brought up and taught to read at home before going on to the grammar school.

Interior of an Elizabethan home, with a cloth-covered "joined" table, i.e. a fixed table made by a carpenter or joiner, as opposed to the older trestle table that could be folded away. As was the custom, the baby in its cradle is tightly bound in swaddling clothes. Master, mistress and both servants are playing cards, for the artist is poking fun at the craze for card games.

The bare interior of a poor man's cottage, with the fire made on the earthen floor but, fortunately, some meat for the pot.

Poorer people's houses

Like wealthier folk, the yeoman-farmer and the tradesman made considerable improvements to their homes. Sometimes, they would pull the old house down and build anew, but, often, they simply added a brick fireplace to one end of the house, building it with seats on either side of the fire.

A chimney made it safe to build an upper room over the parlour and, instead of a ladder, a short staircase might be added or a spiral one built round a strong post.

Corridors and passages were rarely used.

Now that glass was cheaper, the sheets of horn and oiled linen which let in so little light could be done away with in favour of bigger windows which had diamond-shaped panes.

The peasant could afford none of these luxuries and his cottage remained as flimsy and comfortless as in medieval times, with a floor of beaten earth and little more besides a bed, table and a few stools and pots.

The Rich and the Poor

Against the glories of Elizabeth's reign must be set the suffering of the poor. Writers and preachers stressed the contrast between the great wealth of the landlords and the dire poverty of the unemployed. After the Black Death, land was cheap and labour scarce, so many landlords acquired large farms and put their land over to sheep.

From 1500, however, the population increased rapidly and the demand for land and food caused prices to rise, while wages remained low. Hence, efficient farmers and yeomen grew richer and the poor became poorer. Squeezed off the land, they drifted to the towns where trade and industry were expanding, but not fast enough to provide work for all.

The government made praiseworthy efforts to deal with this situation by empowering Justices of the Peace to levy a poor-rate, to fix wages and to provide opportunities for work but, while these measures and the much greater help that came from benevolent citizens did something to relieve poverty, they could not supply what was really wanted—greater production and more jobs.

Art for the rich: a portrait miniature by Nicholas Hilliard, the greatest exponent of this exquisite art form.

Magnificently gowned, an Elizabethan aristocrat—one of the Chalmondley sisters—nurses her first-born.

A group of well-dressed ladies, three of them wives of rich burghers, while the one on the right is probably a farmer's wife.

The cause of much of the trouble—low-cost sheep which needed only one ill-paid shepherd to tend them, whereas, previously, the land had given employment to many workers: from Spenser's *The Shepherd's Calendar.*

Farming changes in the sixteenth century

The old system of farming depended on tradition and co-operation. Landlord and villagers had to agree on the best ways to cultivate their strips and to share the common land but, when land became plentiful and labour was scarce, no-one was hurt if a man acquired extra strips and farmed as he pleased, or if he decided to put his land to grass and keep sheep.

With the sixteenth century rise in population and land shortage, there was no going back to old methods. On the contrary, the process of change speeded up.

Shrewd landlords could raise rents and buy up neighbouring farms; by "engrossing" land, they would save on labour by putting two or three farms together, and the hated enclosers would acquire, by fair means or foul, the common land where the villagers had grazed their animals.

The Poor Law

These changes brought prosperity to the bigger farmers and yeomen, but the husbandmen, who produced only enough to feed their families, fell on hard times. A bad harvest would ruin them and, forced off their land by being unable to pay the rent, they would join the bands of ragged unemployed.

Eventually, it became necessary to compel the rich to help the poor and, by the Poor Law of 1601,

Hop-picking, 1574, from a book on the cultivation of hops (used in brewing), a crop newly introduced from Flanders.

parish overseers were to levy a rate on land in order to relieve the helpless, to provide work for the able-bodied, to apprentice poor boys to a trade, and to erect houses of correction for the vagabonds. Though far from perfect, Elizabeth's Poor Law was a great step forward in social justice.

Part of a field map of Feckenham Manor, Worcestershire, made in 1591, showing one of the open fields, much of which is still divided into strips, but several bigger holdings are evident. "DD" indicates the holdings of Ralf Bowes, clearly a thriving farmer.

Shakespeare's Theatre

Shakespeare's genius could flower in Elizabeth's reign because of the public's tremendous enthusiasm for plays. Yet, London had its first theatre only in 1576—Burbage's "Theatre", closely followed by the "Curtain". Previous to that, people had enjoyed the plays put on by strolling players in inn-yards and town-squares. Since actors were regarded as vagabonds, they tried to place themselves under the protection of some lord; they had names like "The Earl of Leicester's Men" or "The Lord Admiral's Men".

At this time, there were no professional actresses and boys took women's parts on the stage. On the south bank of the Thames was Bankside, famous for its taverns, shows and bear-baiting, and here several new theatres were built, including the "Globe", where Richard Burbage was the star actor, playing the lead in many of the plays which Shakespeare wrote for their company. Between them, they helped to make the theatre respectable and were invited to perform for the Queen at Greenwich. The Puritans, however, strongly disapproved and managed to close the theatres down for a number of years.

The engraving of William Shakespeare from the First Folio of his plays, printed in 1623.

The Bard of Stratford

Born at Stratford-on-Avon in 1564, the son of a glove merchant, Shakespeare attended the local grammar-school, and, as a young man, went to London and became an actor with the Lord Chamberlain's Men.

His gift for writing plays—he wrote at least thirty-six—brought him such success that he was able to buy the best house in Stratford. He died there in 1616.

A sketch made in 1590 of the stage of the Swan Theatre, where many of Shakespeare's plays were performed.

An Elizabethan theatre

In Shakespeare's day, a theatre consisted of a number of galleries surrounding an open "pit", where the common people and apprentices stood. The stage jutted out into the pit and, towards the back of the stage, two pillars supported a roof with a trap-door through which "gods" could descend.

Beneath the roof, an inner stage, which could be curtained off, served for indoor scenes, while the tower, on which the flag flew, could become a castle from whose heights the sound-effects men could fire a cannon for battle-scenes or produce thunder and lightning for a storm.

Left: the earliest known illustration to one of Shakespeare's plays—Henry Peacham's drawing of 1594, showing a scene from *Titus Andronicus*, a play about revenge, set in ancient Rome.

The Globe Theatre, opened in 1599, at Bankside. The flag shows that a play will be performed that afternoon and, when all is ready, a trumpeter will appear on the tower and blow a fanfare.

Cockfights and Dancing

The English Renaissance was at its peak during Elizabeth's reign, having reached the island like ripples on a pond, spreading outwards from Italy to Spain, France and the Netherlands. This was a flowering of literature, art and music, a sudden outburst of creative energy which drove men not only to write, to play, sing and build splendid houses, but to sail the seas and seek for new knowledge of the expanding world—activities in which the English had hitherto been extraordinarily backward.

The Elizabethans were pre-eminently a young people. Only rarely did anyone live to reach the age of seventy, like Elizabeth herself and her great minister, William Cecil, and this youthfulness accounts for the dashing boldness, often amounting to recklessness, of so many enterprises.

It also accounts for the people's love of sport and boisterous amusements, of practical jokes (they liked mazes and concealed fountains that squirted water on passers-by) and even, perhaps, of cruelty. Life was short and, though "melancholy" was a fashionable state of mind, it might as well be merry. They were passionate, lively people who lived life to the full.

Masques

Masques grew out of medieval Court revels and became entertainments in which lords and ladies themselves took part. The best poets and musicians of the day would produce a theme, and the masque, staged in a great house, would use elaborate scenery, lighting and effects unknown to public theatres.

In Elizabeth's reign, masques were popular at Court but the cost and Puritan disapproval caused them to go out of fashion.

A masque in the Great Hall of an aristocratic house where some of the gentry, disguised by masks, are about to entertain the others. At Court, masques became so elaborate that a Revels Office was set up to deal with the organisation of these costly spectacles.

Sports and pastimes

Besides cock-fighting, people enjoyed the cruel sport of bear-baiting at the Bear Garden on Bankside, where fierce dogs were set upon a captive bear or bull.

More civilised sports were bowls, quarter-staff matches and wrestling-bouts, though football was still a riotous encounter with practically no rules. Hunting and hawking remained aristocratic pastimes and archery was still highly popular: the Queen herself was an expert.

Indoor games included chess, draughts and backgammon, but many people also had a passion for dice and for the newly-introduced card-games—another activity on which the Puritans frowned.

Cock-fighting, a popular sport in which birds, armed with artificial spurs, were specially trained for combat.

The Queen's Court

Where the Queen went, the Court moved with her—to Greenwich, Cambridge, Nonsuch Palace or the home of some great lord—and set the pattern of entertainment and culture. Elizabeth would take part in debates in Latin and, at Kenilworth, she hunted, danced in the gardens, watched plays and a fabulous water-pageant. But a refined taste in music and poetry did not prevent her from watching a bear-baiting.

Queen Elizabeth dancing at Court, probably with Robert Dudley, Earl of Leicester. She practised daily, for dances like the lively Galliard and the slow, stately Pavane, were complicated. More than one of the Queen's favourites was said to owe his advancement to his dancing skill.

The Armada

Philip of Spain's aim in life was to wipe out Protestantism and he had meant to deal with England ever since his wife Mary died. At one time, he offered to marry Elizabeth but she remained elusive and he was kept busy by his vast empire and his rebellious subjects in the Netherlands.

The English vexed him for years—robbing his ships, helping the Dutch and trespassing in the waters of the New World—but at last events seemed to have turned in his favour. He had seized Portugal's wealth, harbours and navy; his General Parma had crushed resistance in the Netherlands and, in France, the Catholics had triumphed over the Huguenots.

The execution of Mary, Queen of Scots, put the seal on Philip's resolve, for she had left him her claim to England's throne. His plan was simple. A great fleet, the Armada, would carry 30,000 men up the Channel, take on board Parma's hard-bitten veterans and land this formidable army on the English coast. Although the expedition was delayed for a year by Drake's brilliant raid on Cadiz, preparations went forward and, in May 1588, the Armada set sail.

Tudor shipwrights designing a new galleon. As Treasurer of the Navy, John Hawkins was chiefly responsible for building the warships that out-manoeuvred the Armada.

A 16th century Mediterranean war-galley of the type much used by Spain. Fast and powerfully armed, it was unsuitable for ocean sailing and Channel warfare.

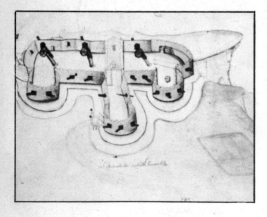

A coastal fort, one of many which the English made ready in 1588. Two armies were mustered and the Queen reviewed her troops at Tilbury.

The rival fleets

With characteristic thoroughness, Philip collected ships, stores, weapons and ammunition. His shipyards worked round the clock, the Mediterranean was scoured for sailors, troop transports were bought in foreign ports and Parma ordered hundreds of barges to be built to carry troops to England.

Portuguese ships were the best available and of the 130 vessels which assembled at Lisbon, 20 were galleons, 44 were armed merchantmen, 8 were Mediterranean galleys and the rest smaller craft and transports. The fleet carried 2,500 guns, most of them short-range cannons, for it had insufficient long-range culverins, but the Spanish gunnery proved to be better than Drake expected.

The English fleet amounted to no more than 36 royal warships, but 150 armed merchantmen and craft of every size were equipped and manned by the coastal towns.

The English handled their ships well and, in the four principal commanders, they had sailors whose experience was far superior to that of the Duke of Medina-Sidonia and his officers of noble birth, who knew nothing of naval warfare.

The two fleets in the Channel: they clashed off Portland Bill, but the Armada kept formation and continued eastwards with the English at its heels.

"God blew and they were scattered"; the Armada flees north (not in such good order as shown here) and the English follow, though their ammunition is spent.

Elizabeth in the "Armada portrait"; at Tilbury, she declared "I know I have the body of a weak feeble woman but I have the heart and stomach of a king, and a king of England too".

The Queen's policy

Until the Armada actually approached her shores, Elizabeth had no intention of fighting Spain if she could possibly avoid it. She hated war, because it interfered with trade and cost far more than it was worth. Hence, though she encouraged her "sea-dogs" and had no hesitation in accepting a share of their profits from raiding the Spanish Main, she pretended to Philip that she knew nothing of these exploits.

For years, she resisted the appeals of her Ministers to send an army to the Netherlands, preferring to dole out "underhand" assistance to the Dutch, while forever hoping that the French would get themselves entangled in a war with Spain, so that the English need not fight.

Elizabeth was no coward; she believed that, in England's interests, it was better to scheme, to tell lies and even to break treaties than to embark upon an official war.

The sea-battle

The main English fleet was at Plymouth, and when the Armada was sighted on July 19th, four squadrons put to sea under Lord Howard, the commander-in-chief, Drake, Hawkins and Frobisher. For a week, they dogged the slow-moving Armada, doing a good deal of damage, but failing to prevent its relentless progress up the Channel.

When Medina-Sidonia, the Spanish commander, anchored off Calais on the 27th, preparatory to making contact with Parma, the situation was critical. The navy's ammunition and food were almost spent and the Spanish fleet was still intact.

Desperate steps had to be taken and, during the night, eight old ships were towed towards the enemy, set on fire, and allowed to drift towards the anchored fleet. The Spaniards cut their cables and, by dawn, the great fleet was scattered along the coast.

A gigantic failure

The English squadrons sailed in, keeping up the attacks until all their shot had gone and Medina-Sidonia had decided on flight. Escape was not easy. There was no friendly port to offer shelter and, battered by a gale, the Spaniards made north to sail round Britain. Many of their ships were wrecked and of the 130 which set out, only 53 returned to Spain. "I sent you out to war with men", said King Philip, "not with the elements."

Setting Sail for America

While the Spaniards prospered in the New World and the French settled in Canada and the Mississippi Valley, the English took little interest in distant seas until John Hawkins began voyaging to the Caribbean. Between 1566 and 1569, he sailed via West Africa in order to buy or capture negroes whom he sold to the Spanish planters.

On his third voyage, Hawkins and his kinsman, Francis Drake, narrowly escaped disaster when the Spaniards attacked them at San Juan. Breathing vengeance, Drake made several piratical voyages and, in 1577–80, sailed round the world to complete the greatest voyage so far made by an Englishman.

After Frobisher had failed to find the North-West Passage, Raleigh and Humphrey Gilbert put forward a scheme to found an English colony in North America. Gilbert perished in a storm but, in 1585, Raleigh sent out a party of colonists to Roanoke Island in the "new land" called Virginia. The project failed miserably, but, in the next reign, Raleigh's dream became a reality when, after a perilous start, Virginia established itself as the first English colony in America.

During the voyage round the world, Drake's flagship, *The Golden Hind,* is towed to her anchorage in the Moluccas or Spice Islands by native galleys.

Indians of Virginia sharing a meal: a drawing by John White made in about 1585.

Sir Walter Raleigh, the courtier and explorer who founded Virginia.

The Virginian settlement

Optimistic reports on the land which the Elizabethans chose to name Virginia encouraged Raleigh to send out his first colonists in 1585. They landed on Roanoke Island but, finding no easy riches, they soon became discontented and, in the following year, were glad to be taken home by Drake.

Raleigh's second expedition, consisting of 150 settlers led by John White, went out in 1587 and fared even worse, for the colonists vanished, probably through starvation or Indian attacks.

However, much had been learned and, in London, the Virginian Company was formed to push on with the project, so that, in 1607, a well-equipped party reached Chesapeake Bay and founded Jamestown in honour of James I. Too many of the settlers were unwilling to work and the colony would have foundered from mutiny, sickness and famine had it not been for the resolute leadership of Captain John Smith. The story of the Indian princess saving his life puts a romantic glow on the fact that he won the Indians' friendship.

When more settlers and supplies arrived, the colony became a permanent settlement but, by 1622, out of 10,000 colonists who had gone out, only 2,000 were alive.

Map showing the sea routes taken by English voyagers between 1566 and 1588, the year of the Armada, whose disastrous course can be seen opposite. Many attempts were made to find a North-West Passage to Asia but this was never a practicable route for ships.

Armada 1588

Davis 1587

Frobisher 1576/77

Newfoundland

Gilbert 1583

Raleigh's Virginia Colony 1585/86

Drake 1572/73

Azores
Islands

Madeira

Canary
Islands

St Augustine

Havana

Cuba

Jamaica

Monte Christi
Isabella
Hispaniola

Sierra Leone
(Slave Coast)

San Juan
de Ulua

Guadaloupe

Hawkins 1566

Hawkins 1567/69

Trinidad

Margarita

Rio de la Hacha

Borburata

Santa Marta

Cartagena

Drake 1579

The Rebirth of Knowledge

The Renaissance caused men to rediscover the ideas of the Ancient World and it also encouraged them to reach out for new knowledge, particularly of nature and of the physical world. There were no clear dividing lines between science and magic, astronomy and astrology, chemistry and alchemy, and the universities still discouraged practical experiments, since all knowledge had to fit theoretical systems worked out by the Ancient Greeks.

Hence, men with enquiring minds were driven to experiment privately; they wrote to each other about their discoveries and built up an international correspondence about science and mathematics.

Scientists tended to be amateurs—doctors, clergymen, pharmacists and so on, who were often encouraged by noble patrons who provided them with instruments and places to meet. Since the universities were not interested, there came into existence a number of scientific societies, devoted to experiment and discussion on subjects that ranged from gravity, magnets and the blood to botany and astronomy.

Teaching the alphabet: a pupil reads from a "horn book", a bat-shaped piece of wood on which the alphabet was pasted and covered with a sheet of horn, so the "book" lasted for generations. Notice two incentives to learning—the apple in the teacher's hand and the birch on the table.

As runs the Glafs, Our Life doth pafs.

My Book and Heart Muft never part.

Job feels the Rod, Yet bleffes GOD.

Proud Korah's Troop Was fwallow'd up.

Lot fled to Zoar, Saw fiery Shower On Sodom pour.

Mofes was he Who Ifrael's Hoft Led thro' the Sea.

Part of a child's alphabet, with the letters accompanied by rhyming jingles containing Biblical references—a form of instruction favoured by earnest-minded Puritans. By Tudor times, almost every town had its grammar school. The main subject was Latin, with some Greek, Hebrew and arithmetic.

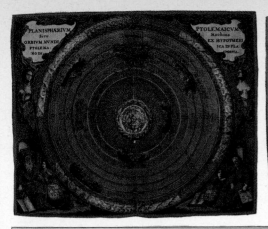
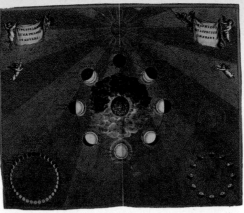

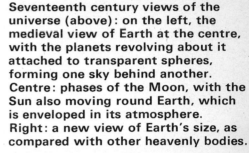

Seventeenth century views of the universe (above): on the left, the medieval view of Earth at the centre, with the planets revolving about it attached to transparent spheres, forming one sky behind another. Centre: phases of the Moon, with the Sun also moving round Earth, which is enveloped in its atmosphere. Right: a new view of Earth's size, as compared with other heavenly bodies.

Scientists of the sixteenth and seventeenth centuries

In 1543, the Polish astronomer, Copernicus, published his belief that the planets, including earth, circle about the sun—a theory that founded modern astronomy.

His work was continued by Brahe, a Dane, who produced a star catalogue and worked with the German astronomer, Kepler, who revealed the movements of the planets and made discoveries in physics and geometry.

In about 1600, in Italy, Galileo perfected a refracting telescope to enable him to study the stars and put forward scientific theories so contrary to established ideas that he fell into dispute with the Church and was tried by the Inquisition.

In England, William Gilbert (1600) produced a study of magnets, and Robert Boyle and Robert Hooke carried out important experiments in chemistry, while William Harvey laid the foundation of modern medicine by his discovery of the circulation of the blood.

Charles II chartered the Royal Society in 1662 and Isaac Newton produced a whole series of discoveries in mathematics, physics and astronomy.

Robert Hooke's handsome microscope of about 1680, an instrument superior to one invented by Leeuwenhoek, a Dutch naturalist; (Galileo also invented a microscope). Hooke used his microscope to study phenomena, such as plant cells, which had hitherto been unknown to man.

The Martyrdom of Ireland

After Strongbow's invasion, Ireland retained a smouldering resentment of the English who occupied the conquered territory known as the Pale and steadily increased their power. However, many of these feudal lords became Irish in almost every respect, obeying no law except that of the ancient tribal system until Henry VIII took a hand in the country's affairs. In an attempt to enforce the Reformation, he closed Irish monasteries and seized valuable relics and ornaments.

Elizabeth's Irish policy aimed at imposing England's system of government, religion, and social customs upon a country which, long divided by clan warfare, now became united in its Catholicism and its hatred of the oppressors. Relations were further embittered by Spanish interference.

After the Earl of Desmond's rising of 1580 had been crushed and his Munster lands settled by English colonists, O'Neill, Earl of Tyrone, made a determined attempt to overthrow English rule and to set up an independent Irish State. He failed, but the death blow to Gaelic Ireland did not finally come until Cromwell's onslaught nearly fifty years later.

Irish troops in the field: English kings found it impossible to make the title "Lord of Ireland" a reality.

Irish clansmen of the 16th century: when Shane O'Neill came to do homage to Elizabeth in 1562, Londoners were astonished by the appearance of his bodyguard, bearing axes, wearing long hair curling over their foreheads and clad in shaggy mantles. Some of the chiefs, promoted to earls, did put on a show of observing English customs.

The ungovernable Irish

Outside the towns and an area round Dublin, the Irish spoke the Gaelic language and clung to their own ways of life. It was a rural society, without towns or villages, and there was no supreme ruler but a number of chieftains, each independent in his own territory.

His followers and kinsfolk supported themselves by cattle-raising and robbery, but they despised merchants and all the values to which Elizabethans attached so much importance—fine houses, furniture, books and a settled form of government.

The Irish set little store on buildings and works of art, preferring spoken poems and small shrines adorned in honour of a local saint.

Henry VIII's Lord Deputy of Ireland, Sir Anthony St Leger, had some success in persuading the Irish chiefs to accept protection of the English Crown in return for recognition of their land titles but this period of comparative peace came to an end in Elizabeth's reign. Attempts to impose English customs and Protestantism on a people who were determined to have neither, led to war and lasting hatred.

O'Neill's rebellion

Educated in England, Hugh O'Neill, Earl of Tyrone, returned to his native Ulster with Elizabeth's favour and support. However, as the pressure of English rule increased, he decided to free his country and set up an Irish State, possibly under Spain's protection.

He united many of the chiefs, defeated the English in 1598 and fended off the expedition led by Essex. Too late and too far away, a Spanish army landed at Kinsale and O'Neill, forced to march across country to join his allies, was defeated by Mountjoy, Elizabeth's new commander.

The submission of Hugh O'Neill in 1603, after the Spanish general had surrendered at Kinsale. O'Neill retained his title and lands, but the clan system was broken and Ireland subjugated.

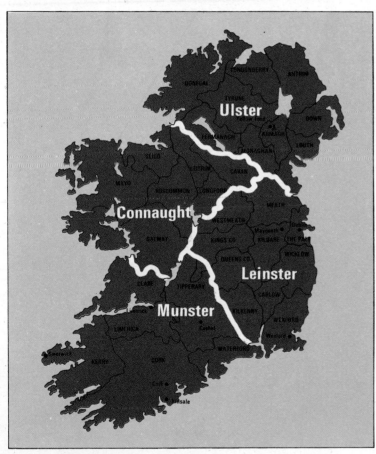

A map showing Ireland divided into counties. The Irishman's loyalty was to his clan chieftain, for, until the arrival of foreign missionaries in Elizabeth's reign, the Church's influence had declined.

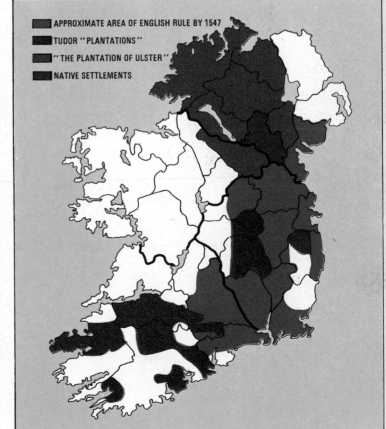

Ireland in the late 16th century, showing the spread of English rule. By settling the Plantations, the government hoped to solve the land shortage in England and extend its rule over the Irish.

The Irish population

Three different groups lived in Ireland. First came the English of the Pale, protected by the Dublin garrison, and of the towns, such as Wexford, Cork and Limerick, whose loyalty was far from certain.

Second came the Anglo-Irish, who had been so long in the country and had mixed so thoroughly with the Celtic population that they had lost all trace of their Norman origin; since they included the great landowners, they made up a powerful group, though their loyalty to the Crown was suspect.

The pure Irish who formed the third group inhabited the poor and remote areas. By planting colonies of Protestant settlers, the Elizabethans hoped to pacify this half-savage island; instead, they united the clansmen and revived the Catholic religion.

King of Scotland and England

In the ninety years that followed James IV's death at Flodden, 1513, Scotland went through an unhappy time. James V, Mary, Queen of Scots, and her son all came to the throne as infants and, during their minorities, the nobles engaged in a murderous struggle for power. French influence was strong, for James V married a French princess and, after his death, she and her advisers ruled the country.

This situation alarmed Protestant England and, in efforts to secure the marriage of Henry VIII's son, Edward, and Mary (James V's daughter), Scotland was twice invaded. For safety, Mary was sent to France and, on her return, she found that John Knox had converted the country to a strict form of Protestantism. This unfortunate woman was eventually driven from the throne and replaced by her baby son.

Bullied and harassed in his youth, James VI gradually asserted the royal authority and did more than all his warlike predecessors to establish law and order in Scotland. In 1603, upon the death of his cousin, Elizabeth, this clever, ungainly Scot became James I of England.

Execution of Mary, Queen of Scots, at Fotheringay Castle: she met her end with brave dignity, saying to the axe-man, "I forgive you with all my heart, for now I hope you shall make an end to all my troubles."

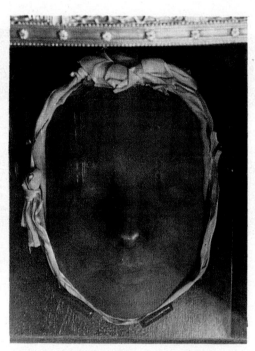

Mary's death-mask: years of imprisonment and ill-health had not obliterated her beauty.

The tragic Queen

Mary, Queen of Scots, daughter of James V and Mary of Guise, was born in 1542, a few days before her father's death.

Sent as a child to be educated at the French Court, she married Francis, heir to Henry II, King of France, who died two years later and, at seventeen, Mary was Queen of France, of Scotland and, she claimed, through her Tudor grandmother, of England too. It was not long, however, before her sickly husband died and the young widow came home to a country she scarcely knew.

In her absence, most of the Scots had become strict Protestants and Mary, brought up as a Catholic Frenchwoman, had little understanding of her people, and no wise counsellors to advise her how to rule.

In choosing a second husband, she made a disastrous mistake, for her cousin, Lord Darnley, proved to be a worthless oaf who murdered her secretary and friend, David Rizzio, and was himself murdered, almost certainly by the Earl of Bothwell. Mary's marriage to this violent ruffian so shocked the Scots that they forced her to abdicate in favour of her infant son.

Mary and Elizabeth

Mary escaped to England, where her cousin Elizabeth kept her prisoner for nineteen years. As her hopes and beauty faded, Mary busied herself ceaselessly in Catholic plots, but her letters were intercepted and when it seemed clear that she approved the assassination of the English Queen, Elizabeth reluctantly signed her death warrant.

A dramatic message

In 1603 came the news for which James had waited so long. At about midnight on 26th March, a horseman named Sir Robert Carey clattered into the court-yard of Holyrood Palace in Edinburgh. Reeling with fatigue—he had ridden from London in less than three days—he demanded to see the King and, when he was admitted to the royal bed-chamber, fell upon his knees and saluted James as King of England, Scotland, France and Ireland.

James, doubting his good fortune, asked for proof that Elizabeth was dead, whereupon Carey showed him a ring taken from the Queen's finger. The two countries were united by a Scottish king on the English throne.

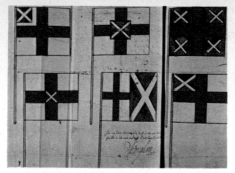

Designs for combining the English and Scottish flags after James Stuart's accession. In fact, none of these was chosen and the Union Jack, as it was called (it was flown from the "jack staff" on a ship's bowsprit), consisted of the cross of St George placed upon the diagonal cross of St Andrew.

Mary Queen of Scots, with her son.

The Scottish King of England

James had a sombre childhood; unloved and deprived of both parents, he was bullied by dour tutors who lectured him incessantly on the duties of kingship.

When he grew up, he gained control by sheer cleverness, for he was astute and exceptionally well-educated, and he worked out a theory that kings were appointed by God. They ruled, he declared, by Divine Right and were free to make and unmake their subjects as though they were "men at chess".

On attaining the English throne, James's good fortune went to his head. So inflated was his notion of his own cleverness, that he dismissed all other men as fools and this conceit brought him into argument with the Puritans.

No fewer than 300 Puritan clergy-men were expelled from the Church and it was not long before the Catholics, too, had every reason to detest the King. Having promised them fair treatment, he allowed them to suffer persecution and heavy fines for non-attendance at Church.

The conflict with Parliament

It was with Parliament that this stubborn autocrat made his greatest mistake.

By deciding to rule without their counsel, James was forced into raising money by devices that brought the Crown into conflict with Parliament.

James I in Parliament. Unlike Elizabeth, James had no flair for managing his parliaments; he lacked regal dignity and could never command the respect of the Members.

In any case, Parliament's mood had changed. The men who sat in the Commons no longer dreaded their sovereign's displeasure but were determined to have a larger share in governing the country, particularly in matters of religion and taxation.

To James, with his theories about Divine Right, this attitude was intolerable and, when Parliament persisted in questioning his conduct of affairs, he resolved to do without it and raise money as best he could.

A Stuart on the Throne

The advent of a new century, with the death of the old Queen and the accession of a Scottish King, brought changes that soon left the Tudor age behind. James and his son, Charles I, pursued their personal interests and tastes, with little regard to the people's mood or Parliament's wishes. Both kings became patrons of the arts, somehow finding the money for artists and architects to produce fine portraits, palaces and elaborate masques. In architecture, the genius of Inigo Jones gave London a number of lovely buildings whose classical style and stone construction were far removed from homely timber and brick.

The greatest triumph of James I's reign may have been the publication of the Authorised Version of the Bible which placed into the hands of Protestants a work of enduring literary value. But, after the Gunpowder Plot, they were not disposed to show mercy or toleration to the Roman Catholics. Parliament and people at large were nonetheless becoming increasingly dissatisfied with the way in which the King and his favourites managed religious matters, finance and foreign affairs.

An unusual windmill in Warwickshire, designed by Inigo Jones. His drawings for a new Palace of Westminster still exist; this would have been one of the most majestic buildings in Europe but, owing to the Civil War, it was never started.

Costume design for a masque, devised at the time when Inigo Jones was in charge of royal entertainments. Producing a masque called for a high degree of artistic and mechanical skill.

Design for a town-house in 1616, a simple elegant building, such as Jones introduced into London.

Inigo Jones—Court architect

As a young man, Inigo Jones spent several years in Italy, where he particularly admired the work of an architect named Palladio, whose style was based on the classical buildings of ancient Rome.

In England, Inigo Jones found employment at James I's Court as a producer of masques and later blossomed out as an architect, designing the Queen's House at Greenwich, churches, buildings and his masterpiece, the Banqueting House, which still stands in Whitehall. Here, he showed a complete mastery of Palladio's style and, in London of the time, his buildings were a startling contrast to anything else in the city.

The Authorised Version of the Bible

Until James I's reign, clergy and people relied on various translations of the Bible—Tyndale's, Coverdale's and others. These versions were full of errors, so James ordered about fifty scholars to prepare a new version.

The main work began in 1607 and the King's Printer produced the Authorised Version in 1611. This was the Bible whose marvellous language became familiar to English-speaking people all over the world and which required no revision for 300 years.

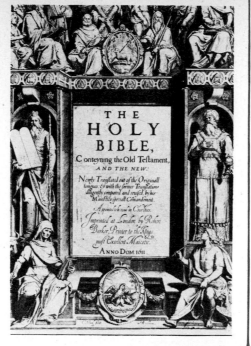

Title-page of the "King James" Bible of 1611, the Authorised Version, which was ordered to be used in all churches.

James I in progress to Parliament, in the last year of his reign, when the foolish old King had to ask for money to make war on Spain.

His daughter and her Protestant husband had been driven into exile by Catholic armies, his son Charles and the favourite Buckingham had bungled a marriage to a Catholic princess in Spain and were now intent on war and a match with Henrietta Maria, a French princess.

James's policy had made England the laughing-stock of Europe and the war with Spain ended in total failure.

Guy Fawkes laying the trail of gunpowder on the night before Parliament was due to assemble.

Earlier that evening, a search-party had already asked Fawkes who owned the firewood in the storeroom, and he had answered cheerfully enough, hoping, by adopting a casual air, to disarm suspicion. However, at eleven o'clock, the soldiers returned and arrested Fawkes, still manfully at his post.

The lantern used by Guy Fawkes on 4th November, 1605.

The Gunpowder Plot

Early in his reign, James I yielded to public outcry and allowed his minister, Robert Cecil, to banish priests and impose severe fines on Roman Catholics.

A small group of hot-heads planned a most violent revenge. Led by Robert Catesby and Thomas Percy, they decided to destroy the King, Lords and Commons at the opening of Parliament.

The conspirators leased the building next to the House of Lords and in its cellar, began to dig a tunnel through the foundations wall. The work was proving difficult, when Guy Fawkes, their explosives expert, discovered that there was a storeroom next door, right underneath the House of Lords.

The tunnel was therefore abandoned and the storeroom hired; in it, Fawkes, a Yorkshireman who had served in the Spanish armies, managed to place thirty-six barrels of gunpowder which he covered up with coals and firewood.

Treachery

While he remained on guard, the other conspirators dispersed to collect arms and horses. One of their number, wishing to save a kinsman from death, sent a letter to Lord Monteagle, warning him to stay away from the opening of Parliament, and when this letter was passed to the government, a search of the buildings led to the discovery of Fawkes and the gunpowder.

The leading conspirators died at bay in a country-house, and Fawkes, who gave nothing away under torture until he knew his companions were dead, went defiantly to his own death on the scaffold.

How the King Raised Money

Throughout the Tudor and Stuart eras, the Crown was perpetually short of money. From royal estates, feudal dues and fines, Elizabeth had an income of about £300,000 a year, but, with all her economies, she had to sell land to make ends meet and she died deeply in debt.

The truth was that the royal income was too small to meet necessary expenses but James I nevertheless believed he had come to a rich country and could therefore spend lavishly. His financial situation became so hopeless that efforts were made to increase customs duties known as tonnage and poundage and the number of monopolies (licences granting the sole rights to sell, manufacture or import certain articles).

These measures were unpopular and, while the obvious solution was to impose a regular system of taxation, Englishmen had a rooted objection to paying taxes. To balance his budget and pay for exceptional expenditure, like equipping an army, the King depended upon grants made by Parliament and when, in Charles I's reign, these grants were refused, he turned to illegal methods of raising money.

A 16th century woodcut showing workers making coins in the Royal Mint.

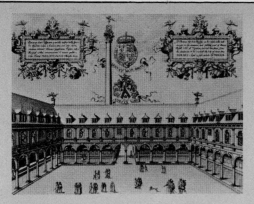

The Royal Exchange, London, built during Elizabeth's reign by Sir Thomas Gresham, a wealthy mercer or cloth-merchant who acted as representative in the Low Countries for Henry VIII and his three successors.

Gresham built the Exchange in order to provide a place where merchants, bankers and brokers could meet to do business.

Tudor finance

The problem of royal finances was an ancient one. The King was supposed to pay all peace-time expenses out of his personal income and he usually met his difficulties by borrowing or by selling Crown Lands. These measures merely reduced the royal income and passed on a worse problem to the next monarch.

When it came to equipping an army for war, Parliament would give its consent to the raising of taxes, but, in practice, it proved difficult to collect the money, for towns and districts would plead hardship and even, on occasion, refuse to pay.

Henry VIII's measures

Henry VII's ruthless methods of raising money aroused such resentment that, to avoid trouble, Henry VIII met part of his vast war expenses out of his "private hoard". When this was exhausted, he obtained money by seizing monastic property and Church lands.

Between 1541 and 1547, he raised a forced loan worth £112,000, two "benevolences" (gifts) that brought in £230,000 to add to parliamentary taxes of about £650,000. Even so, he had to sell Crown lands for £600,000 and he made about a million pounds by debasing the coinage.

Henry's measures postponed the introduction of regular taxation and stored up tremendous problems for Elizabeth and for the Stuarts who followed her.

James I's problems

Early in the reign, a merchant named Bates refused to pay customs duty on a cartload of currants; Parliament and other merchants who objected to the tax on tobacco supported him, but the King's judges found that it was the royal prerogative to levy such duties.

Short of money as usual, James's Treasurer immediately increased the duties on all kinds of merchandise. The extra revenue might well have freed the King from parliamentary control, so the Commons offered him a "Great Contract", whereby he would receive £200,000 a year in place of duties and ancient dues. This was only half the amount that the Court required and the scheme fell through, with bad feelings on both sides.

James tried to raise funds by a "benevolence" but only a small sum came in, and he was reduced to selling peerages for £10,000 each. Nevertheless he managed to meet most of his expenses and, by avoiding war, to rule without Parliament.

At the end of his reign, however, he allowed Buckingham to involve the country in war with Spain, so that, on his accession, Charles I faced a Parliament that grudgingly voted inadequate funds and talked angrily about their grievances. By sending them home, he closed the first scene of the tragedy which ended twenty-four years later on the scaffold.

William Noye (1577–1634) (above), lawyer, who advised Charles to levy Ship Money from inland counties, a tax which Hampden refused to pay.

Cover of a copy of John Pym's speech (above) attacking Charles for taxing the country without Parliament's consent.

A portrait of Charles I (left), whose quarrel with Parliament over taxation was one of the main causes of the Civil War.

Crown and Parliament Clash

The clash between King and Parliament had been building up for many years. By adroit management, Henry VIII and Elizabeth had kept their parliaments in subjection, but the Stuarts never evoked the same awe in Members who were now determined to take a share in governing the country.

They resented the theory of Divine Right and the Stuarts' addiction to favourites. Mostly Protestant, with a strong body of Puritans, the Commons stood for enmity to Spain, harassment of Roman Catholics and reduction of royal perogative. On these issues, they clashed with the King. Certainly, they obtained their war with Spain and it ended in grotesque failure; they disliked Charles's marriage to a Catholic princess; they loathed his friend Buckingham, and dreaded his chief servant, Thomas Wentworth.

Their grievances multiplied. The King raised taxes without their consent, imprisoned men without trial and kept a standing army. After eleven years' rule without Parliament, the issue was clear—personal rule or parliamentary government—and when neither side would yield, the outcome had to be war.

Charles I in the House of Commons, 1642, when he went in vain to arrest the Five Members (John Pym and four others) who had opposed him so hotly.

Charles was an extraordinary character; dignified, kind, artistic, and convinced that he behaved honourably, he was incurably two-faced and quite incapable of keeping his word. A more ruthless man would have won the Civil War; a more sensible one would have made peace.

Trial of strength

Charles's first Parliament met in an angry mood. Shamed by the disasters of the Spanish war, they vented their rage on Buckingham and, to save his friend, Charles dismissed them. When they met again, they presented the Petition of Right, a list of grievances which Charles promised to redress, without any intention of keeping his word. Once again, he sent the Members home. Eleven years later, the Short Parliament met for twenty-three days, just long enough for Pym to pour out a torrent of complaints.

Then, in 1641, the Scottish War brought in the Long Parliament, the assembly which raised the armies that fought the King.

In 1629, Charles became so exasperated by Parliament's criticism that he ordered the House to dissolve. The Speaker was about to rise when, as this picture shows, he was held down in his chair to enable the excited Members to pass three resolutions condemning the King's policies.

The two sides

At the start, the nation did not want war. Only in London, where Pym and the Puritan preachers had whipped up excitement, was there any violent feeling. However, as the war developed, men found they had to take sides and, in every town and village—and even within families—some were for King and some for Parliament.

Generally speaking, the centres of trade and wealth supported Parliament—London, the South and the East, with the larger towns and the sea-ports. Country districts, the North, the West and Wales, were largely Royalist, but there were exceptions and men and places sometimes changed sides. Catholics and Anglicans were mostly for Charles, while Puritans and nonconformists generally supported Pym.

A broadsheet of 1641, lampooning the downfall of the King's friends and policies—one of the pamphlets which Pym encouraged to fan popular feeling.

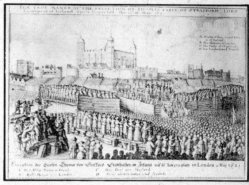

Thomas Wentworth, Earl of Strafford, served Charles so forcefully in Ireland and the North, that Pym resolved to destroy him, lest his methods be turned on Parliament. Above are scenes from his trial and execution before a vast crowd, after Charles had basely abandoned him.

"King Pym"

The man who, above all others, opposed the King and brought about the Civil War, was John Pym, a prosperous gentleman from Somerset.

From the time he entered Parliament, he took the lead in attacking Buckingham and Wentworth and in pressing Parliament's grievances.

A powerful speaker, and a master of propaganda, Pym worked with fanatical zeal to stoke the fires of opposition, publishing his own speeches, promoting a petition for a new parliament and stumping the countryside to arouse public opinion.

To further his aims, he did not scruple to use the rabble to keep London in a state of ferment and, while speaking incessantly of liberty, he had some Members expelled and others sent to the Tower.

When war broke out, Pym's cool-headed management of affairs sustained his party during the early set-backs and his death in 1643 was a tremendous loss to the parliamentary cause.

The Great Rebellion

After eleven years of personal rule, Charles was forced to summon Parliament through a foolish quarrel with Scotland. He and Archbishop Laud ordered the Scots to adopt an English-style Prayer Book and when they refused, Charles called a Parliament in order to obtain money to fit out an army. But while Parliament voiced its grievances, the Scots captured Newcastle and demanded money.

In came the Puritan-dominated Long Parliament which, under Pym's leadership, brought Laud to prison and Wentworth to his trial and death. Not content with these triumphs, Pym now drew up a great list of the King's tyrannies, a declaration so insulting that Pym seemed to have overreached himself and a Royalist party began to take shape.

Feeling himself in a stronger position, Charles resolved to act, and with 400 Cavaliers, went to arrest the five Members who had given him so much trouble. They escaped, and this final piece of folly convinced many that Charles meant to overthrow Parliament. Both sides now began to count their supporters and to look to their weapons.

Iron cannon-ball fired at the Battle of Naseby.

Weapons in the Civil War

The opposing armies consisted of cavalry armed with pistols and swords and footsoldiers carrying muskets or sixteen-foot pikes. Usual armour was a leather coat or jerkin, iron breast- and back-plates and an open-faced, "lobster-tailed" helmet, often with three face-bars.

The pikemen were needed to protect the musketeers, who were now greatly to be feared, for the guns were more accurate and musket-balls would pierce almost any armour.

In this cartoon of 1642, the war is compared to a dog-fight between Roundhead and Cavalier. In fact, it was not fought with bitter savagery but more in a spirit of regret, and there was no slaughtering of civilians and hardly any sacking of towns.

Cavaliers and Roundheads

The word "Cavalier" came from "cavaliero", a Spanish trooper, popularly regarded as the brutal oppressor of Protestants, so "Cavalier" was first heard as a term of abuse for the young bloods who swaggered about with drawn swords posing as royal guards, in the turbulent days when Pym was rousing the Londoners.

"Roundhead" was the Royalists' contemptuous term for the crop-headed apprentices who were always game for any riotous demonstration. The word fitted the Puritan parliamentarians, whose short hair, prim dress and sober colours contrasted with the flowing locks and lace collars of the Cavaliers.

But it is easy to exaggerate these distinctions. The gentry on both sides dressed very much alike and the parliamentary footsoldiers tended to be better turned out than the King's infantry who were often ragged and wretchedly armed.

A pro-royalist stained-glass window in Farndon Church, Cheshire, showing the King emerging from his tent and a selection of weapons including a musket and musketeer's belt with small bottles of gun-powder.

Banners of the officers of the Parliamentary army. Colonel Lambert became a general second only to Cromwell; Ireton married Cromwell's daughter and subdued the Irish with great severity; Stamford was accused of cowardice.

The course of the war

Hostilities began with the indecisive Battle of Edgehill, 1642, though Prince Rupert could have dashed on the capital, had Charles given permission. When he did advance, his army was repulsed at Turnham Green. Events in 1643 went mostly to the King, for the Royalists came near to winning the war.

The tide turned in 1644. Cromwell's cavalry won a major victory at Marston Moor and, next year, Parliament gained a decisive one at Naseby. Though Montrose fought gallantly in Scotland, the war was virtually over and, in 1646, Charles surrendered to the Scots. Handed over to Parliament, he tried playing a double game, but the New Model Army put down a Royalist rising and Charles was executed in 1649.

After this, Cromwell crushed resistance in Ireland, defeated the Scots, and, in 1651, overwhelmed Charles II's army at Worcester, the last battle. In the long run, Parliament's superiority in money, cannon and infantry was decisive.

Frontispiece of a Royalist book, "recounting the sad events of the late unparalleled Rebellion", with pictures of outrages committed by the Parliamentarians.

The Execution of Charles I

After Naseby, the Royalist cause collapsed, and Charles soon found himself without commanders or troops to carry on the struggle. In May 1646, he gave himself up to the Scots, who, finding him too tricky to deal with, passed him on to Parliament.

Charles was amused to find Parliament and its Army at loggerheads and, by playing off one against the other, he fully expected to regain the throne. From captivity at Hampton Court, he escaped to the Isle of Wight, only to be made prisoner by the castle governor. However, he was soon in touch with the Scots, promising to establish their Presbyterian religion in England and to suppress other forms of worship.

When Cromwell got wind of these plans, he vowed to bring "that man of blood" to account and, as soon as the Scots had been dealt with, Charles was brought to trial. Public opinion was now on the King's side but no-one could act, for Cromwell and the Army held complete power and they had decided that, by God's Will, Charles should die. On January 30th, 1649, Charles I, King of England, was beheaded in Whitehall.

Oliver Cromwell
A country squire, cousin of John Hampden and Member of Parliament for Huntingdon, Cromwell was forty-three when he became a Captain in the Parliamentary Army. Though he had no military experience, the poor quality of the troops at Edgehill disgusted him and he returned to East Anglia to recruit and train a body of men.

At Marston Moor, his cavalry defeated Prince Rupert's hitherto invincible Horse, and the New Model Army came to be dominated by Cromwell and his Ironsides. Naseby established his reputation as a General and his subsequent victories showed him to be a master, not only of cavalry tactics, but also of deploying infantry and artillery.

A broadsheet showing Charles a prisoner at Carisbrooke Castle. He had gone there believing that Colonel Hammond, the Governor, was a Royalist but, as usual, his judgement was faulty and Hammond kept him prisoner.
Two rescue attempts failed, and Charles remained on the Isle of Wight until taken to London for his trial.

The velvet-covered chair on which Charles I sat during his week-long trial in Westminster Hall.

John Bradshaw, President of the court which tried the King, wore this steel-lined hat for protection.

Charged with high treason, by a court whose 68 members represented barely half the number summoned by the Commons, Charles showed great dignity in refusing to answer his accusers.

When, prior to pronouncing the death sentence, Bradshaw claimed to speak for the people of England, Lady Fairfax, wife of Parliament's Commander-in-Chief, cried out, "Not half, not a quarter . . . Oliver Cromwell is a traitor!"

A contemporary picture showing the King's execution and the people's distress. His head was held up with the words, "Behold, the head of a traitor!" But, in that moment, Charles became the Royal Martyr.

The execution of the King

On the morning of January 30th 1649, Charles was brought from St James's to Whitehall. Snow was falling and he had told his sergeant to bring him an extra shirt to wear, lest the cold made him tremble as though from fear. "I fear not death," he said, "Death is not terrible to me. I bless my God that I am prepared."

Cromwell was finding great difficulty in holding his supporters together, since even those who had signed the death warrant were now aghast at what they had done; however, with the soldiers, Ireton and Harrison at his elbow, he had no doubt that his orders would be carried out.

At one o'clock, Charles stepped through a window of the Banqueting House onto the scaffold set against its wall. His voice could not reach the crowds kept back by ranks of soldiers, so he spoke calmly to those standing nearby and then knelt down at the block.

When the executioner held up the severed head, a great groan burst from the crowd, "such a groan", wrote an eye-witness, "as I never heard before and desire I may never hear again."

Cromwell's Iron Hand

With the King's execution, a Republic called the Commonwealth came into existence that was to be governed by a Council of State, chosen by the Commons. The Council had first to put down a mutiny in the army, where some revolutionary agitators, called "Levellers", gained influence and, next, to order Cromwell to Ireland. Here, he crushed the Irish Royalists with appalling severity, before returning to defeat the Scots at Dunbar and the Prince of Wales at Worcester.

Events had made Cromwell the most powerful man in the country and, certain that God had specially chosen him for the task, he took on the burden of leadership. Like many another successful general, he found politics a difficult and exasperating game. The remnant of the Long Parliament was useless, yet free elections would bring in the Royalists, so he found himself compelled to rule without Parliament.

He became Lord Protector, a King in everything but name, whose authority rested, not upon the people's consent, but upon military force. The man who had played the major part in destroying Charles I, took on the role of tyrant.

Cromwell at the siege of Drogheda, 1649. He entered the town and ordered all armed men to be killed. About 2,000 perished, including the English commander, all the priests and a few civilians.

Cromwell in Ireland

In 1641, a rebellion broke out in Ireland and, during the Civil War, the King's representative, the Earl of Ormonde, sometimes fought and sometimes wooed the rebels, hoping to win them to the Royalist cause.

Charles's execution caused Ormonde to make terms with the Catholics and, while he laid siege to Dublin, English Royalists arrived and Prince Rupert's fleet appeared off the coast. At this point, Cromwell set out for Ireland with an army that regarded itself as the Lord's avenging instrument sent to chastise the barbaric Irish. Ormonde threw his best troops into Drogheda, but the town was stormed and its garrison put to the sword.

A month later, Cromwell took Wexford with a slaughter that was equally bloody. Cromwell's cruelty and seizure of Catholic lands have never been forgotten.

The Common wealth ruleing with a standing Army.

An anti-Commonwealth satire, portraying Cromwell as a dragon who has devoured parliament and enchained the people. His diet includes the monarchy, nobility, laws, bishops and English rights.

Cromwell removed judges from office, and, like Charles I, dismissed parliaments and levied taxes without consent. Meaning to rule well, he became a greater tyrant than Charles had ever been.

"Begone, you rogues, you have sat long enough!" Cromwell dissolves the Rump in 1653, having called in his soldiers to turn Members out.

Cromwell and Parliament

At first, Cromwell tried to work with the remnant of the Long Parliament, "the Rump", but, finding its main aim was to keep itself in existence, he angrily sent the Members packing.

In its place came "Barebone's Parliament", whose "saintly" reforms aroused such ridicule that it soon handed its power back to Cromwell. Now he was nominated Lord Protector and, once again, he assembled a parliament, only to find it challenging his power, as earlier parliaments had challenged the King.

After only five months, therefore, he dismissed them and ordered Major-Generals to rule the country in military districts. They, too, were turned out and the next parliament came up with the offer of the crown for Cromwell. He declined the title, but still found it impossible to work with parliament; he was ruling without one when he died in 1658.

The Speaker's Mace, symbol of his authority and of Parliament in session. Eyeing it, Cromwell asked, "What shall we do with this bauble?" and, turning to a soldier, added, "Here, take it away."

The New Armies

The seventeenth century saw the triumph of fire-arms over armour. It also saw the rise of standing armies, of a professional officer-class and of war studied as a science. Cannon made castles obsolete, and strongpoints came to be defended by earthworks—ditches, mounds and banks—since earth absorbed cannon-balls where stone walls disintegrated.

Armies became more mobile and professional, with intensive drilling of the soldiers so that commanders could move forces and change formations at a signal. In battle, regiments of infantry consisted of musketeers protected against cavalry by pikemen and reinforced by field-guns firing as rapidly as the musket. Improved weapons allowed the men to load and fire faster; in three ranks, one kneeling, one stooping, one standing, they fired a volley and retired to allow the next three ranks to take over. Then, in attack, they advanced "at push of pike and butt end of musket".

Cavalry, essential for scouting, protected the army's flanks and rear and, in the charge, moved in tight, disciplined lines, to present a solid mass to the enemy.

A picture from *The Art of Gunnery*, a military handbook published in 1608, showing siege-guns in action against a fort.

Blow of your loose powder.

A musketeer warned to blow away any spilt gunpowder before firing his weapon—an engraving from the New Model Army's instruction book.

War in Europe

Compared with the Civil War in Britain, continental warfare was immensely sophisticated and far more savage.

In their attempt to crush the Dutch, the Spaniards first developed a standing army and comparatively modern tactics.

In the Thirty Years' War, a religious struggle which devastated Germany between 1618 and 1648, it was Gustavus Adolphus of Sweden who perfected infantry and cavalry tactics and was the first to make full use of artillery in the field.

An aristocratic officer-class emerged in France and Prussia, with military schools to train cadets for an army career.

Siege warfare

The decline in importance of castles did not lead to a decline in the art of fortification. The capture and defence of key towns remained one of the major objects of a campaign, especially in small countries like the Netherlands, where armies operated in confined areas.

Military engineers adapted their methods to meet the increased efficiency of artillery, and men like Vauban, Louis XIV's expert, became such masters of siege warfare that campaigns tended to become almost static.

Complicated fortifications were linked by trenches, and forts were constructed with low earth walls of immense thickness to serve as platforms for guns.

Towns would be protected by a series of such forts, and the besiegers, in their turn, would construct similar systems of forts. Siege cannons fired a forty-pound ball and mortars were designed to fire an explosive ball high into the air so that it would land inside the fortifications.

An illustration from a French manual of artillery, 1613, showing a gun-battery set up for besieging a town, with the guns on plank floors so they could be easily moved (they had to be drawn back for muzzle-loading). The battery is protected by earth-filled wicker cylinders.

Notice the musketeers on top of the sandbags, and pikes standing ready to repel a counter-attack.

The Puritans' Commonwealth

The name "Puritan" came into use in Elizabeth's reign to ridicule those who wanted to "purify" the Church of so-called popish abuses. To some Protestants, it was not enough to have thrown off the Pope's authority; they wanted to abolish bishops, regular clergy, the Prayer Book, images, candles—anything that came between a man and his God.

In Scotland, Protestants influenced by Calvin, a Frenchman, became known as Presbyterians, because their leaders were not bishops but presbyters or elders, and this type of church government became widespread in both Scotland and England. But many other forms of Puritanism emerged; there were Congregationalists, Baptists, Unitarians, Quakers and various groups, known as Separatists and Independants.

All Puritans were united in opposition to the Church of England and most believed in a form of plain worship, based upon the Bible and led by a minister of the congregation's own choosing. They devoted themselves to leading godly lives and took what seemed perhaps an undue pride in avoiding the sins of the wicked.

Puritan influence

The actual number of Puritans was never very great but, for a time, their influence was enormous.

During the Civil War, they executed the King and Archbishop Laud, abolished the bishops and the House of Lords; in America, they founded a Bible Commonwealth in New England.

There were many sects. Some Puritans, like Pym, wanted to stay in the Church as reformers, but many others founded their own small congregations. Cromwell was one of the Independants who believed he was following the direct instruction of the Scriptures.

Puritans chose their own minister and paid him; he preached the Word but they, too, were God's elect, "saints", who had joined the congregation only after a searching examination.

Though it is easy to sneer at their earnestness and preoccupation with sin, most Puritans put their beliefs into practice—they were sober, industrious, charitable people. Their virtues were many and their failings were usually conceit and intolerance.

A 17th century meeting of Quakers, the Society of Friends, founded by George Fox. This form of Puritanism has no ministers or set services; Quakers believe in silent worship and the "light within". Their beliefs, especially the unlawfulness of war, made them unpopular and they suffered persecution.

Puritan writers

The Puritans' opposition to church music and to such ungodly pleasures as theatre-going and dancing meant that some of the arts were closed to them. Writing, however, was not, and the greatest poet of the century, John Milton, was a Puritan scholar and ardent admirer of Cromwell.

As a young man, Milton threw himself into the Parliamentary cause, writing fierce pamphlets, including a grandiose propaganda piece justifying the execution of Charles I. At the Restoration, he was lucky to escape with only a short spell in prison.

John Bunyan (1628–88) served in Cromwell's army and became a Baptist preacher. After the Restoration, he was imprisoned for 12 years.

Now blind and disillusioned, he wrote "Paradise Lost", an epic poem that expressed his disappointment that his countrymen had cast away the chance of true liberty. This was followed by "Paradise Regained" and by "Samson Agonistes", in which the blind Samson (Milton himself) throws off despair and finally destroys his enemies.

Milton's friend, Andrew Marvell, was a gifted writer and poet but he cannot compare with the other great Puritan writer, John Bunyan, the son of a tinker, who went to prison for his preaching and wrote in prose of tremendous power and simplicity, "The Pilgrim's Progress", the story of Christian's perilous journey to the gates of Heaven.

The Puritan way of life

Before the Civil War and after the Restoration, Puritans frequently had to suffer for rejecting the established Church. Some went to prison or fled to Holland, and many settled in New England.

Their objection to a state Church was partly that it included everyone, the wicked as well as the godly, and they believed themselves to be God's elect, specially chosen to live in close fellowship with their congregation, as in the early days of Christianity.

With their intense beliefs, they often quarrelled with one another, but, nevertheless, they tried to live up to Puritan ideals. The Puritan father had clear duties towards his wife, children and servants; he led them in prayer, provided religious instruction and taught his children to read the Bible at an early age.

In everyday life, there was no idleness, swearing, lying or frivolous

The beginnings of toleration: a 17th century painting showing men of varying religious beliefs discussing their views. This was still only an ideal, though Milton and many others, thought all men, except Roman Catholics, should be free to worship as they chose.

amusements; in business, there were no unjust prices, high wages, money-lending or cheating. Above all, the Sabbath was holy, a day given over entirely to worship, sermons and reading the Scriptures.

The Early Americans

After the Spaniards had built a vast empire in Central and South America, Europeans from other nations had to content themselves with lands further to the north. Here, they found no fabulous riches but a country where it was possible to live by farming, fishing and trading in furs.

Raleigh's project had failed but, in 1607, the English arrived in Virginia and, during the next thirty-three years, they founded four settlements—at Plymouth, around Massachusetts Bay, in Connecticut and on Rhode Island.

Between these areas, the Dutch had settled in the Hudson River valley, founding the "New Netherlands", with its capital, New Amsterdam, on Manhattan Island. Rivalry with Swedish fur-traders along the Delaware led to the Swedes being driven out but, in 1664, the Dutch themselves received similar treatment from the English, whose colonies now stretched in an unbroken line along the eastern margin of the continent.

It was not possible, however, to dislodge the French who, since 1534, had steadily gained control of the northern coastline, of the St Lawrence River and the Great Lakes.

The building of Jamestown (above), the first permanent township in Virginia, named after James I; in theory, all land settled by Englishmen belonged to the King.

John Smith, founder of Virginia (left). His determination and aggression made him many enemies.

A colonial pioneer

After a series of incredible adventures fighting the Turks, Captain John Smith set out in 1606 with 150 pioneers on a venture organised by the London Virginia Company.

At Chesapeake Bay, Jamestown was laid out but, owing to sickness and quarrelling, the colony would have perished, but for Smith. Taking over leadership, he traded with the Indians for food, explored the countryside and the Bay and, when captured, was saved from death by the Indian princess, Pocahontas.

Slowly, the colony prospered and Smith became its President in 1608, but his brusque answers to the London Company's demands for greater profits and gold, led to his recall.

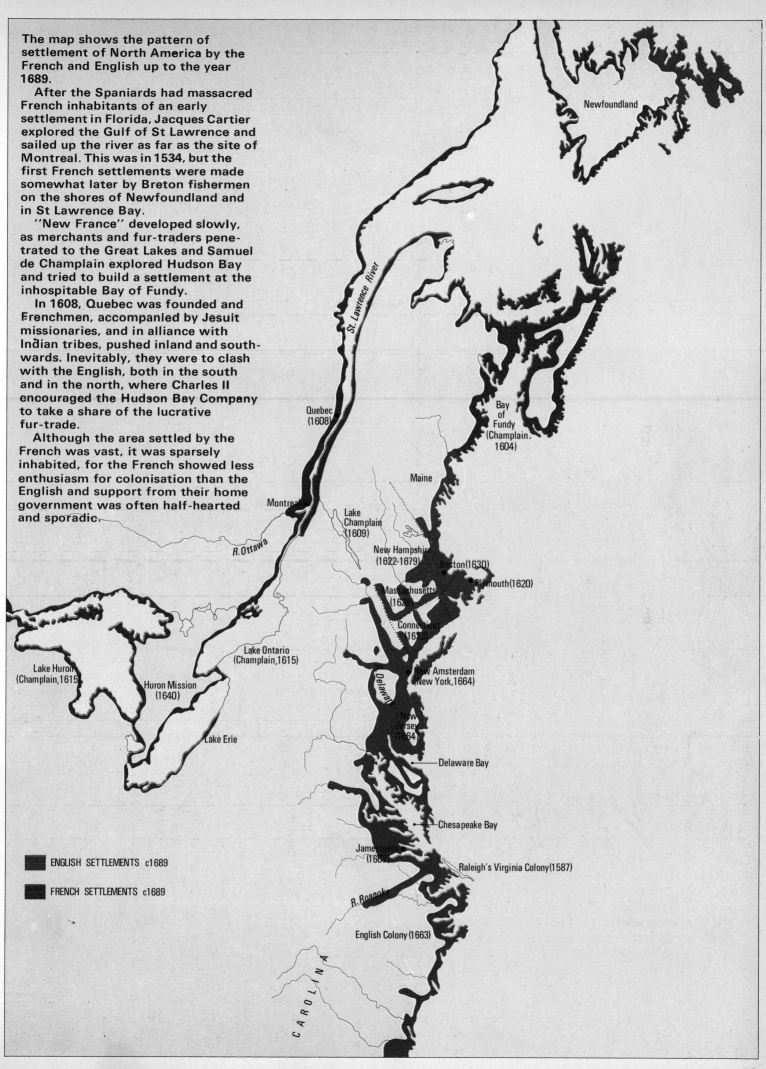

The map shows the pattern of settlement of North America by the French and English up to the year 1689.

After the Spaniards had massacred French inhabitants of an early settlement in Florida, Jacques Cartier explored the Gulf of St Lawrence and sailed up the river as far as the site of Montreal. This was in 1534, but the first French settlements were made somewhat later by Breton fishermen on the shores of Newfoundland and in St Lawrence Bay.

"New France" developed slowly, as merchants and fur-traders penetrated to the Great Lakes and Samuel de Champlain explored Hudson Bay and tried to build a settlement at the inhospitable Bay of Fundy.

In 1608, Quebec was founded and Frenchmen, accompanied by Jesuit missionaries, and in alliance with Indian tribes, pushed inland and southwards. Inevitably, they were to clash with the English, both in the south and in the north, where Charles II encouraged the Hudson Bay Company to take a share of the lucrative fur-trade.

Although the area settled by the French was vast, it was sparsely inhabited, for the French showed less enthusiasm for colonisation than the English and support from their home government was often half-hearted and sporadic.

Newfoundland

St. Lawrence River

Bay of Fundy (Champlain, 1604)

Maine

Quebec (1608)

Montreal

Lake Champlain (1609)

R. Ottawa

New Hampshire (1622-1679)

Boston (1630)

Plymouth (1620)

Massachusetts (1628)

Connecticut (1635)

Lake Huron (Champlain, 1615)

Lake Ontario (Champlain, 1615)

Huron Mission (1640)

New Amsterdam (New York, 1664)

Delaware

Lake Erie

New Jersey (1664)

Delaware Bay

Chesapeake Bay

Jamestown (1607)

Raleigh's Virginia Colony (1587)

R. Roanoke

English Colony (1663)

CAROLINA

■ ENGLISH SETTLEMENTS c1689

■ FRENCH SETTLEMENTS c1689

The New Life in America

In 1603, England did not possess a single colony. Sixty years later, the framework of a British Empire had been built, with colonies all along the east coast of North America and on several islands of the West Indies. Why was there this sudden urge to go and settle in distant and largely unknown parts of the world?

Hope for a better life was one powerful incentive, for the prospect of land grants attracted many landless labourers and small farmers in England. The monarchy usually favoured colonisation, not only to keep up with rival nations but to promote trade and increase the customs revenues on incoming goods. Merchants and bankers who provided ships and stores for the settlers naturally looked for profits in return and were indeed often unrealistic in demanding searches for gold and routes to the South Seas.

Many of the settlers, like the Pilgrim Fathers, went out to escape the penalties for following their own religious views, and there were some who had no choice about emigrating, for deportation was an easy way of getting rid of undesirables.

The people of Rhode Island cheer the sight of their Charter in 1663. Religious quarrels in Massachusetts had caused them to found a new settlement.

A Royal Charter: this one was granted by Charles II to the Hudson Bay Company, headed by Prince Rupert. Its main business was fur-trading.

Founding the colonies

The founding of a colony required royal permission, for subjects were not free to leave the country as they pleased and all lands overseas belonged in theory to the King. It was therefore essential to obtain a Royal Charter which might be granted to a company or to an individual.

The Pilgrim Fathers waited anxiously for James I's permission to settle in America and, in the next reign, Charles I gave Lord Baltimore power to govern the new colony of Maryland.

Why the King wanted colonies

To some extent, the King's interest in colonies was financial; it was, after all, his duty to promote his subjects' well-being and encourage trade, though, in fact, the colonies generally proved to cost more than they produced in return.

However, prestige was important; other monarchs possessed colonies and the King of Spain was drawing a fortune from his overseas empire. Religion was a difficulty, for settlers were supposed to conform to the established Church, so, in the case of the Puritans, the Anglican bishops had to be soothed.

The London Virginia Company

The Royal Charter was usually granted to a "joint-stock" company, a new method of raising money, by which people bought shares in hope of eventually reaping a profit.

For the second charter of the London Virginia Company in 1609, 583 subscribers put up money to support the colony but, alas, they never made a profit and, by 1624, the Company was bankrupt. Its charter was withdrawn and Virginia, with Bermuda and New England, came under direct rule of the Crown.

Who were the settlers?

Colonists were mostly humble folk of small means—artisans, shop-keepers, farm labourers and the like, though there were generally a few gentlemen in the party.

The southern colonies such as Virginia and Maryland, had a greater variety of people and classes than the Puritan colonies of New England, and John Smith complained bitterly about the work-shy ex-servants and down-at-heel swaggerers who went out to Virginia in hope of an easy life.

How they lived

Most settlers had to face hunger and great hardship while the colony was establishing itself. Trees had to be felled, land cleared for crops and the town built by the settlers' own hands.

The country provided ample timber and stone for building, but in New England, a stony soil and harsh climate made life so perilous that one of the colony's greatest problems was the abnormal rate at which people fell sick and died.

The Indians were friendly at first, but as they came to realise the menace of the white man, their attitude changed and, in 1622, occurred the first massacre.

The colonists had to find ways to pay for such necessities as iron goods and cloth. Virginia could export tobacco but New England produced little to export and, for many years, this question of how to trade remained a dire problem.

The landing of the Pilgrim Fathers at Plymouth, Massachusetts on December 11, 1620. Under their leaders, John Carver and William Bradford, these 102 Puritans or Separatists had sailed from Plymouth, England, on 6th September in the *Mayflower*. By the end of the first bitter winter, only half the company remained alive.

Anglo-Dutch rivalry

Shortly after the English settled in Virginia, the Dutch came exploring the valleys of the Hudson and Delaware rivers. They built forts and founded New Amsterdam as their capital, where they engaged chiefly in the fur trade.

Conflict over this valuable trade developed with both the Swedes and the English, but whereas the Dutch were able to drive out the Swedes in 1651, the English were too numerous to eject and their settlements now lay both north and south of the New Netherlands.

The squabbles continued until, shortly after the Restoration, Charles II sent a force to annex New Amsterdam, and Peter Stuyvesant, the last Dutch governor, surrendered the town.

A Dutch ship of the West India Company arriving at New Amsterdam (later re-named New York).

In 1622, the Dutch States-General granted a charter to the Company (an offshoot of the thriving Dutch East India Company), giving it a monopoly of trade between Holland and the coasts of North and South America, with West Africa as well. The Company was also to develop the settlement of New Netherland, whose capital, above, was founded on Manhattan Island.

America's Indians

At the outset, the settlers lived on friendly terms with the Indians. The white man's possessions, notably blankets, weapons and liquor, were so attractive that the Indians quickly learned how to acquire them by barter. The Europeans wanted furs and, in the early days, food, and it was only through the Indians' friendliness that the settlers at Jamestown and Plymouth survived their first winters.

Nevertheless, suspicion developed on both sides. Many of the settlers saw nothing un-Christian in exterminating the heathen savages, and the Indians, for their part, began to realise that the white man menaced their way of life. It is curious to note that the first massacre of settlers occurred just when a scheme was afoot to open an Indian college.

Trading continued; many hunters and trappers had Indian friends, and the Dutch, French and English all made alliances with various tribes (Iroquois friendship was an important factor in the successful advance of the English settlements) but, beneath the surface, lay a basic antagonism between a primitive people and the land-hungry Europeans.

The Indian way of life

When the Europeans arrived in North America, the native inhabitants were mostly following a Stone Age way of life. The Indians, as they were called from Columbus' belief that he had reached a part of India, numbered about one and a quarter millions and dwelt in tribes, of which some of the best-known were the Iroquois, the Blackfeet, the Algonkins and the Cherokees.

Living by hunting, fishing and primitive agriculture, the Indians had no domestic animals except dogs, no wheeled vehicles, towns or written language. Their weapons and implements were mostly made of wood and stone, though some use was made of copper from the Lake Superior region.

Hunting, particularly with nets and snares, provided them with food but they also grew maize (Indian corn) in crude fields, enriching the soil by placing small fish at the roots of the plants.

They knew how to make fire, pottery, canoes and tent-houses which could easily be transported when they moved to fresh hunting-grounds. For their chief, the tribesmen would build a "palace" of branches and bark.

Indian beliefs and crafts

In their religion, the Indians believed in a Great Spirit who had power over all forms of life, and most tribes had their own demi-god and great respect for magic.

American Indians playing a game resembling hockey. Attempts to convert the Indians to Christianity were mostly unsuccessful.

Arts and crafts included painting on skin, bone and pottery, embroidery, bead-work, feather decoration and carving of stone and wood, including the totem-poles set up for the spirits. They enjoyed music, especially singing to the accompaniment of drums, whistles and rattles.

John Smith and Pocahontas

During the first year at Jamestown, Smith traded with the Indians and, having learnt their language, took a native guide with him on an expedition into the interior. The man led him into an ambush, and he was taken before Great Chief Powhatan.

Smith's bold demeanour and display of a pocket-compass greatly impressed the Chief, until he became alarmed by the stranger's boasting of King James's ships and armies. Smith was about to be clubbed to death when Pocahontas, the Chief's daughter, dashed forward and begged her father to spare his life.

After Smith's release and return to Jamestown, Pocahontas seems to have been responsible

An Indian village, with a palisade: another painting by White, who was sent to Virginia by Raleigh.

for the friendly relations that developed with Powhatan's tribe. Having adopted Christianity, she married John Rolfe and accompanied him to London where she was received as a celebrity.

Indians fishing, one of the vivid water-colours of John White, 1585.

The signing of the peace treaty between Penn and the Delaware Indians. Voltaire called it "the only one never sworn to and never broken".

The Quakers in America

William Penn, son of an admiral, became a Quaker and was imprisoned for his views. After his release, Charles II made him a grant of land in America where, in 1681, he founded the colony of Pennsylvania as a haven for persecuted Quakers.

His capital he named Philadelphia—"the city of Brotherly Love". Because the land was fertile and the Quakers worked hard, the colony prospered from the start and attracted shiploads of immigrants, many of them Germans and Dutch.

As pacifists, the Quakers were

opposed to fighting the Indians and Penn made a series of treaties with them for purchase of land—treaties which were never broken by either side.

London Day by Day

By Charles II's reign, one Englishman in fourteen was a Londoner. The city was the largest in Europe; no other town in England was one tenth the size; it doubled its population between Elizabeth's death and the Restoration. This rapid growth brought many problems.

Suburbs sprang up outside the city and beyond the control of the Lord Mayor; gardens vanished, as property developers put up houses at high rents; slums multiplied and, despite Charles I's attempts to impose controls, the capital became ever more crowded, criminal and dirty. The new coaches and hackney-carriages choked the streets and the increasing use of coal fires made the atmosphere filthy.

The kingdom was top-heavy when most of its business and industry were concentrated in London (four-fifths of total exports went from the Thames); the country gentry flocked in and so did the unemployed and the fortune-seekers. Nowhere else was there such bustle, wealth, pleasure and intrigue. This above all others was the place where a man could express his grievances and stand on his rights.

Watermen rowing a party of gentle-folk across the Thames. In the background is London Bridge, built in the 12th century, with a road and shops on top. The river ran so swiftly between the piers that "shooting the bridge" was a perilous experience which nervous citizens would avoid by disembarking above the bridge.

A blind water-carrier with his dog. People did not realise the danger of impure water and used river water into which the city's drains emptied.

London life

The streets were noisy, crowded and stinking. Though there existed regulations against dumping rubbish in the streets, these were rarely observed or enforced, and the most effective form of street-cleaning was heavy rain that carried the filth away to the river.

Water-sellers still sold water of dubious quality, though, since 1613, a canal called the New River brought clean water from Hertfordshire and a reservoir had been built at Islington.

By road and river

Sedan chairs became the fashion, hackney coaches plied for hire and private citizens began to own coaches and "flying chariots". This extra traffic made the city more congested than ever and the best way to get about was by river, where boats of every size carried goods and passengers. London Bridge was the only bridge across the river, but there was a ferry at Lambeth.

Street-traders, bawling their wares and ringing bells, sold milk, cherries, cakes, mouse-traps, coal, pots, old clothes and dozens of other goods which are now bought in shops.

A few watchmen patrolled the streets at night but it was risky for anyone to walk alone, so gentlemen carried swords and, when going home late, hired a coach or employed a link-boy to walk ahead with a lighted torch.

A cresset-bearer, carrying a cresset (iron container) of burning coals or wood to light the streets.

Entertainments

After the Restoration, theatres reopened, with performances in the afternoon; cock-fighting and bear-baiting were still popular and Londoners could now enjoy themselves out of doors in the royal parks, in the Mulberry Gardens and at Vauxhall, where they could stroll about, listen to music, drink wine and watch the horse- and chariot-racing.

Food for the capital

The Londoners' food came in by boat, waggon and "on the hoof", as drovers brought their flocks and herds along the roads leading to the capital. Foodstuffs were sold in the markets and in certain streets like Bread Street and Milk Street.

Englishmen were now eating more vegetables and fruit, and market gardens developed to the north and the west; their produce was sold in the market near St Paul's, and also in the new Square at Covent Garden. Potatoes were not popular, except in Ireland.

Smoking tobacco, a habit introduced to London in the 1560's and becoming widespread after the colonisation of Virginia.

Food and drink

Bread, beef, beer and cheese were the people's staple food, but a much greater variety began to appear on the tables of the well-to-do. Oysters, anchovies, fish of every kind, gooseberries, artichokes, oranges and raisins became popular, and Samuel Pepys mentions in his Diary, "We had a fricasée of rabbit and chickens, a leg of mutton boiled, three carps on a dish, a great dish of a side of lamb, a dish of roasted pigeons, a dish of four lobsters, three tarts, a lamprey pie, a dish of anchovies, good wine of several sorts."

The city was full of cook-shops where complete meals were cooked and supplied to houses, and also of taverns where men met to do business and exchange news over their "morning draught" of wine or beer, though coffee was soon to be all the rage.

The poor fared less well, for prices had risen steeply, and they lived largely on bread, herrings, cheese, and cheap meats, like sheep's heads and pig's trotters. Most of them believed that vegetables were "windy" and unfit to be eaten, except in broths.

A beggar family in London, where the authorities were burdened by paupers who drifted in from the country.

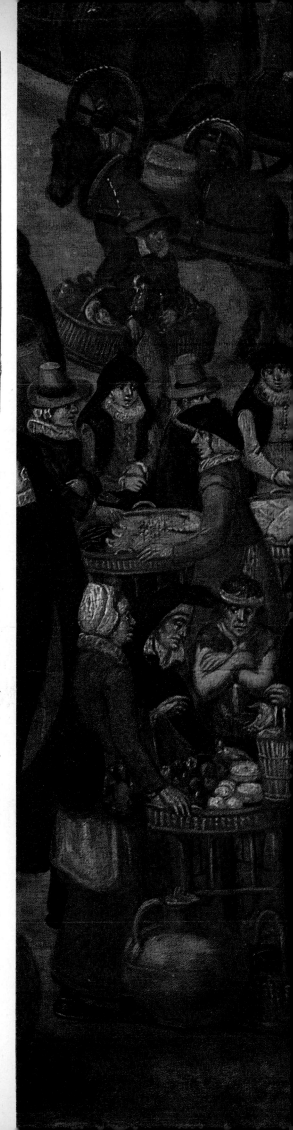

London housewives shopping (right): practically all the buying and selling of foodstuffs was done, not in shops, but in open-air markets. Inspectors checked weights of loaves and cheeses and accuracy of scales, but all kinds of cheating were prevalent.

Printing and the First Newspapers

Until the invention of printing, education was available only to the privileged few. Religious teaching was largely by word of mouth, news was passed on from one man to the next and all written information had to be copied out by hand.

When printed books did arrive, there was no sudden flooding of the market, but a gradual spread of knowledge. People's thinking became better informed; with a copy of the Bible in front of him, a man might begin to form his own views of the Church's teaching; with a pamphlet in his hand describing the government's action, he might decide to demand his rights.

Kings and parliaments, therefore, regarded books and news-sheets with active dislike. Printing was controlled, licensers supervised the publication of news and those who offended authority were liable to find themselves sentenced to flogging, prison or even to the gallows. When these strong measures went out of use, governments still tried to curb the press by taxing printed publications, but the English people's "thirst for news" has never abated from the appearance of their first newspaper to the present day.

William Caxton, whose passion for books led him to take up printing.

The early printers

Johann Gutenberg printed his great Bible at Mainz in 1455, using a secret process which was movable type. This "mystery" soon became widely known, and William Caxton, an English merchant living in Bruges, studied the new craft; in 1476, he brought a press to London. Here, he printed more than a hundred books.

Early printers had to "compose" separate letters, called "type", into words in a frame, the type was inked and sheets of paper were pressed, one at a time, on top of the wet type. Woodcut illustrations, hand-

A page from Caxton's *The Game and Playe of Chesse*, printed in Bruges in 1474, before he went to London to set up his press at Westminster.

coloured after the printing, were used over and over again.

Only two sizes were printed at first—*folio* books whose pages were about 16 inches by 12, and *quarto*, when the pages were folded in half to make a book 12 inches by 8. One more folding eventually produced a third size, *octavo*, which is 8 inches by 6.

The growth of publishing

So long as books were handwritten and made of parchment, they remained the costly possessions of monasteries and of a few wealthy nobles. With the founding of universities, more books came into use and were supplied by "stationers", so called because their shops were stationary, as distinct from the packs of wandering pedlars.

The invention of printing brought a gradual increase in the output of books, especially textbooks, religious and classical writings and books on medicine, astronomy and mathematics. There was also a lively market for romances, as well as for plays, poetry and travellers' tales. Books usually appeared in paper covers and buyers would order a bookbinder to make a special cover for each, often in gorgeously decorated leather.

The government nearly always looked on books with suspicion, so printing was only allowed in London, Oxford and Cambridge.

Writers in print

A bookseller was publisher, printer and bookseller combined. He paid the author a fee, not a royalty, and, since his sales did not allow him to pay well, most writers were wretchedly poor, unless they had the support of some wealthy patron. (Milton received only £5 for "Paradise Lost".)

Publishing by subscription—that is by getting a number of people to promise to buy the proposed book—brought better terms for some writers, and the poet Dryden, for example, received £1,200 for his translation of Virgil.

Before the invention of printing: a 14th century bookseller displays a handwritten book to his customers. By this time, paper-making was widespread in northern Europe and an organised book trade had developed.

The 30. of May.

WEEKLY NEVVES FROM ITALY, GERMANIE, HVNGARIA, BOHEMIA, the Palatinate, France, and the Low Countries.

Translated out of the Low Dutch Copie.

Jor Robinson

LONDON:
Printed by E. A. for *Nicholas Bourne* and *Thomas Archer*, and are to be fold at their Shops at the *Exchange*, and in *Popes-head Pallace*.
1632.

Headlines of the first newspaper printed in England, 1622, giving news of the Thirty Years War in Germany. A similar paper had appeared earlier in Amsterdam, the home of religious toleration and many English exiles.

NUMB. 52.

THE NEWES

PUBLISHED FOR THE

SATISFACTION & INFORMATION of the PEOPLE.

WITH PRIVILEGE.

JULY 6, 1665.

By order from the Right Honourable the *Lord Arlington* principal Secretary of State to His Majestie, I am commanded to publish the following advertisement to satisfy all persons of the great care of the Right Honourable the Lords of His Majesties most Honourable Privy Council, for prevention of spreading of the infection. Who by their order dated the one and thirtieth day of *May* last past did authorise & require the Justices of the Peace for the County of *Middlesex* and City and Libertie of *Westminster*, or any five of them, to treat with *James Angier*, Esq., upon his offers of certain Remedies and Medicaments for stopping the contagion of the Plague & for disinfecting houses already infected, &c. And whereas *Sir John Rabington*, Knight & Baronet, His Majesties Lieutenant of the Tower, *Sir George Charnocke*, Knight, His Majesties Serjeant at Arms in Ordinary, *Humphrey Weld, Thomas Whartin, Joseph Ayloffe, Robert Jejon, James Norfolk*, Serjeant at Arms attending the Honourable House of Commons, and *William Bowle*, Esquires, Justices of the Peace for the said County of *Middlesex*, did at the desire of the said *Angier* & the inhabitants in the house of *Jonas Charles* in *Newton Street*, in the Parish of *St. Giles* in the Fields, in the said County, permit one *Richard Goodall*, servant of the said *Angier*, with his Medicaments, to enter the said house on *Thursday*, the 8th of July, instant. After four several persons had dyed full of the spots out of the said house and eight more remained therein, whereof two were infected with the Plague. And whereas upon examination of several witnesses upon oath before the said justices, proof was made—that upon application of the said Medicaments there, and in several other houses, no person had dyed in any of the said houses since the same was therein used. And whereas in persuance of the said Order the said Justices upon the 12th instant did report to the Lords of the Council, to whom the prevention of spreading the infection of the *Pestilence* is referred, their proceedings thereupon. And whereas upon reading the said *Justices* report and the proposals of the said *Angier*: as also of his several Certificates from foreign parts, for proving the happy success of the said *Angiers* Remedies in stopping the Infection in *Lyons, Paris, Stronbourg* and other cities, the said Committee of Lords did

The Newes, published in 1665, in which the government informs the public of steps taken to prevent the Plague from spreading. News-sheets had flourished during the Civil War, until Cromwell imposed a tight control, and the flood of papers which gushed forth at the Restoration was soon stopped by Charles II's officials. The news of the day, often mere gossip and rumour, had to be picked up in taverns and coffee-houses.

The King Returns

Cromwell died in 1658, naming as his successor, his son, Richard. But "Tumbledown Dick", as he was called, possessed neither the will nor the capacity to rule England, nor could he appeal, like his father, to the army's loyalty. Finding no support from any quarter, Richard very sensibly threw up his post and retired into private life.

This left the Army in charge, but while its officers and men still favoured a republic, who was to govern? The Rump Parliament commanded no respect but a new parliament would assuredly bring back the King. Gradually, all but the die-hard extremists began to see that there was no alternative to the old order of King, Lords and Commons.

A leader emerged in the person of General Monk, commander of the army in Scotland, a man who had kept quiet and aloof from the generals' squabbles. With his army, he marched towards London, slowly enough to convince the generals that public opinion was totally against further bloodshed. When they stepped off the stage, the way was clear for a new parliament to ask Charles II to return from Holland.

A marble bust of Charles II, which brilliantly depicts the cynical gaze of a man for whom life had come to mean pleasure and self-preservation.

In poverty-striken exile, Charles had learnt to trust no-one, but to face the world with an easy smile and a witty retort. Cool, affable and highly intelligent, he preferred pretty women and amusing company to the business of state.

But beneath this easy-going surface, he was utterly determined to keep his throne and, if possible, to rule as he pleased.

How the King came back

Once Cromwell's son had resigned, the only stumbling-block to the King's return was the Army. The generals recalled the Rump Parliament and tried to insist that it governed according to their wishes; the Rump refused and was replaced by a "committee of safety". When soldiers began collecting taxes with drawn swords, public anger exploded, and, as the soldiers found themselves universally hated, their morale collapsed.

General Monk marches south

Everything now depended upon General Monk, commanding a disciplined army in Scotland. Cautiously, he announced his obedience to Parliament's authority and ordered his men to march south. In London, he restored the Rump but soon found that this republican clique refused to disband itself or to admit the excluded Members.

London greets the King

Amid mounting excitement, while people roasted rumps of beef in the streets, Monk withdrew the guards at Westminster, so that the excluded Members could take their seats in the House. They had already agreed to dissolve parliament and, in the election that followed, the one condition that made a candidate's return certain was his support for the King's restoration. In May 1660, when Charles II rode into London, the people greeted him with an outburst of joy.

Revenge for the death of Charles I: a picture showing the execution of some of the regicides by hanging, drawing and quartering.

From Charles II's "free and general pardon", only those who had condemned his father were excluded. Fifty-nine "regicides" had signed his death-warrant and, of these, a third were dead, a third had fled and twenty remained to face trial. Only nine were executed and the others died in prison.

The bodies of Cromwell, Ireton and Bradshaw were dug up, hanged and thrown on the dunghill, while their heads were exhibited to public gaze.

Charles II presented with the first pineapple ever grown in England.

Foreign tastes

When, as an exile, young Charles appeared at the French Court, he seemed awkward and shy. This did not surprise the French, for they regarded the English as uncouth boors. By the time Charles returned, he was a polished wit with gracious manners, and the English Court, taking its tone from its master, became both gay and civilised.

In Puritan eyes, it was also decidedly wicked. The music, dancing and theatre-going, the sight of the King gossiping with a bevy of gorgeous ladies, while the courtiers gambled and drank, filled even the pleasure-loving Pepys with shocked astonishment.

Elegant fashions

French taste and elegance replaced Puritan austerity. Elaborate decoration was all the rage; upholstered chairs appeared, as well as such fashionable novelties as day-beds, looking-glasses and lacquered cabinets from the East. Coaches and smart "chariots", based on French models, became the latest form of transport.

Close contact with Holland also influenced English life; Dutch experts came over to advise on drainage, brick-making and the building of "pleasure boats".

The Queen's dowry included Bombay, Tangier and a share in the Portuguese eastern trade, so that one-time luxuries, such as oranges, melons, lemons, wines, silks, tea and coffee came to be enjoyed by the well-to-do classes.

The Popish plot

The Restoration promised religious toleration to everyone except Roman Catholics but, despite Charles II's distaste for religious fervour, the Cavalier Parliament insisted on passing a number of laws known as the Clarendon Code of 1662. Nonconformists and Catholics were excluded from public life unless they conformed to the Church of England. The laws were not strictly enforced but, in 1673, there occurred a violent anti-Catholic outburst. People feared Catholic France and the numbers of Catholics in high places, and when a scoundrel named Titus Oates came forward with so-called revelations of a "Popish Plot" to murder the King, panic-stricken fury seized the public.

Blameless Catholics were beaten up and executed, and the King, with his own secret leanings towards Catholicism, could only stand aside and wait for the storm to die down.

Three playing-cards recording events of the Popish Plot. Left: Titus Oates informs the King of the conspiracy to murder him, and put James, Duke of York, on the throne. Charles never believed Oates's story. Centre: Oates swears his tale to Sir Edmund Berry, a magistrate, who was presently found murdered. Right: Coleman, the Duke of York's Catholic secretary, is examined in prison.

Fire and Plague

Early in Charles II's reign, London suffered two disasters, so terrifying that some Puritans declared God was punishing the sinful for their wicked behaviour since the Restoration.

In 1665, an outbreak of bubonic plague paralysed the capital. Plague was nothing new, for it visited most large cities every summer and severe outbreaks had occurred during the reigns of James I and Charles I. On this occasion, it seemed especially terrible, partly because people now lived in greater comfort and security, and partly because chronic overcrowding made treatment and burials almost insuperable problems.

Thousands died and many more fled to the country until, with the coming of winter, the infection declined but, in the following year, another calamity struck. Fire broke out near London Bridge, and destroyed a great part of the city, though not the ramshackle hovels outside the walls. Extremists blamed the Catholics but commonsense soon asserted itself and everyone pressed on with the work of rebuilding, not alas, to the spacious plans of Sir Christopher Wren, but at least in a style worthy of a great capital.

A terrified Londoner flees the Plague.

A contemporary list of parishes showing weekly totals of Plague deaths.

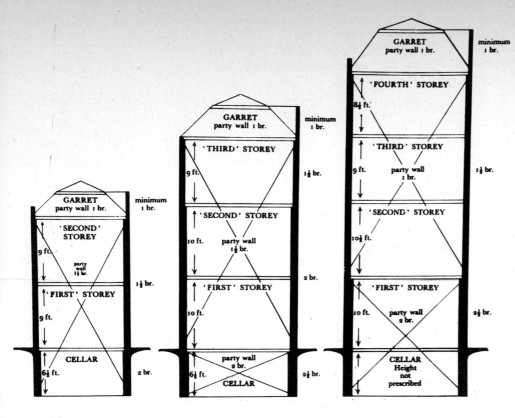

Sections through the three permitted types of houses (left); the smallest for "by-streets and lanes", the next for "streets and lanes of note", and the tallest for "high and principal streets."

Rebuilding after the Fire

By Royal Proclamation, the city was to be rebuilt in brick and stone. Plans for a truly noble city had to be abandoned because of the impossibility of making a thorough survey and compensating all who would have lost their property.

However, many streets were made wider and three types of brick houses were required. All building work in the country was forbidden in order to attract workers to the capital and a tax on coal provided money to rebuild St Paul's and the city churches.

The Great Fire, 1666

The fire started accidentally at night in a bakers' shop in Pudding Lane and, by morning, the flames, driven by an east wind, were leaping across the narrow thoroughfares and devouring street after street of wooden houses.

The river was low, fire-engines were few and primitive and, although the authorities tried pulling down houses in the path of the fire, it overtook all their efforts and Pepys came across the Lord Mayor wringing his hands, "like a fainting woman".

People could do little, except try to escape by boat, but the King and the Duke of York ordered sailors to blow up houses with gunpowder to create gaps which the flames could not cross.

This demolition work and a change of wind caused the fire to die out on the fifth day. Very few deaths had occurred, but more than 100,000 persons were homeless, 13,000 houses had been destroyed, together with 89 churches, St Paul's Cathedral, London Bridge, scores of warehouses and many public buildings.

Within a week, Christopher Wren and John Evelyn had put in plans for rebuilding the city and the King speedily appointed commissioners to plan the vast undertaking. One difficulty was the total lack of insurance, so that many citizens were ruined, but most of them managed to rebuild their homes and businesses with astonishing speed and, by 1672, the whole area was thick with buildings.

An Italian artist's impression of the Fire of London. Old St Paul's, a gigantic Gothic pile, can be seen left centre and the Tower of London, whose gunpowder store was threatened, is on the extreme right. Sir Christopher Wren's work was mostly advisory, though he designed many of the new churches and St Paul's Cathedral, started in 1673.

The Wits and the Wags

The Restoration of Charles II released the people from the fears and restrictions of the long Puritan regime. All over the country, maypoles were set up and the King's coming was greeted with music and dancing, with loyal toasts and an almost frantic determination to make up for lost time.

The King set the example, allowing the public to see him at his pleasures, at the theatre, riding, playing tennis, sailing his yacht, opening the gambling on Twelfth Night and roaring with laughter at the anecdotes of Court wits.

The people followed suit. Card-playing came back into fashion, musical entertainments enlivened the evenings, theatres played to packed houses, with people chuckling at spicy comedies which would have shocked the Puritans. Taverns and coffee-houses buzzed with gossip about the goings-on at Court, where Charles's mistresses were glamorous celebrities and fortunes were lost and won at cards. There were those who shook their heads at such frivolous licence but most people were reacting against the gloom which had enveloped England during the rule of Cromwell and the "saints".

Samuel Pepys, a kinsman of the Earl of Sandwich, who rose from a humble clerkship to a most influential post at the Navy Office.

John Evelyn looks on dourly as the King chats with Nell Gwynne, a popular actress, whom he, like the Londoners, genuinely loved.

Antony Wood (1632–1695), scholar and historian of Oxford, who was frequently in trouble for his biting opinions on politics and religion.

Pepys' Diary

Pepys' Diary gives a fascinating account of his public and private life. Written in secret code, it covers only nine years, 1660–1669, but it deals with the Restoration, the Plague, the Fire of London and Pepys' own rise in the world.

He recorded what he saw and heard at Court, in the Admiralty Office and in and about London, setting down his private thoughts, his occasional mean tricks and vanity, his love of music, theatre, merry company and pretty women.

Evelyn's Diary

John Evelyn, a clever, learned and slightly pompous man, was a Royalist who took care to stay abroad until after the Restoration. He, too, kept a diary, which is less entertaining than Pepys', but full of information about the interests of a seventeenth-century gentleman.

Sober and industrious, he de-deplored the sinfulness of the Court, though he knew everyone of importance and was always busy with public affairs, plans for rebuilding the city, and science.

Wood's Diary

Antony Wood, who amassed a great library and wrote a vast amount about the history of Oxford and its university, kept a diary covering the same period as Evelyn's and Pepys'.

It is not so interesting or as well written as theirs, but it has a sarcastic stinging tone, as when he noted how the Puritans had changed their ways and how the courtiers who came to Oxford during the Plague were "rude, vaine, nasty and beastly".

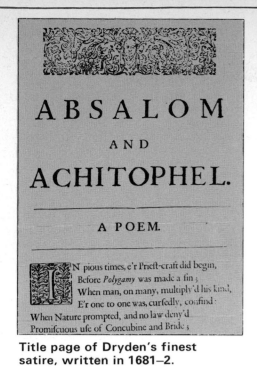
The arts in Restoration England: the theatre

The theatres, closed since 1642, re-opened when Charles II granted Killigrew and Davenant a virtual monopoly of putting on plays in London. Their companies performed at the Cockpit, Drury Lane, at the King's Playhouse and, presently, at the Duke's House in Lincoln's Inn Fields. These theatres were roofed in and had drop-curtains and movable scenery.

Shakespeare was now out of favour, except when his plays were "adapted" by Davenant and others, for comedies, tragicomedies and satires by Beaumont and Fletcher, Ben Jonson and Congreve were more to the public's taste.

Literature

Although Milton and Bunyan wrote their best-known works in this period, they were Puritans out of tune with its light-hearted tone. Wit and a kind of clever mockery were much admired, but of the writers and poets fashionable at Court, only Dryden possessed first-rate ability.

Painting

English painting could not compare with that of Italy, France and Holland. Foreign artists came to work in England, where interest in painting was growing and the King, who had recovered part of his father's marvellous art collection, encouraged artists. Indeed, Charles II must be given much credit for the revival of the arts in England.

An ale-house in which citizens gather to take their "morning draught" and to hear the news of the day, in conversation and by news-sheet. They could breakfast there, eat the "ordinary", a mid-day dinner at a fixed charge, and sup late at night, for taverns were open all hours and were essential meeting-places for business and merriment.

Coffee-houses

Coffee-houses began to take over the tavern's role and, by the end of the century, were said to number 480 in London. A customer paid a penny to enter, to read the news and join in the talk. He could order what he liked, write letters and have his mail addressed there, use the servants to run errands and leave word for his acquaintances with the girl at the counter.

Among well-known coffee-houses were Friar's, the Jamaica, Will's, the Bay-tree, the Bedford, the Cocoa-tree, the Turk's Head, Old Slaughter's and White's. Many had regular customers who formed groups of writers, politicians, booksellers, sea-captains and so on.

Modern Science is Born

Interest in science was greatly stimulated by the Restoration, for Charles II readily encouraged men with enquiring minds. This passion to find things out by practical experiment—by dissecting bodies, for example, or, like Francis Bacon, stuffing a dead chicken with snow to investigate refrigeration—was not favoured by the universities.

Amateur scientists, interested in anything from fossils and freaks of nature to planets and anatomy, refused to be satisfied with theories handed down from the ancient Greeks, so they experimented, wrote to each other and formed societies to discuss their interests. From 1645, a group of Englishmen began meeting regularly in London and Oxford and, in 1662, Charles II granted them the charter that founded the Royal Society. Though disappointed by the monarch's failure to provide them with money, the members (14 nobles, 5 clergymen and 18 doctors) investigated all kinds of phenomena, carried out weekly experiments and collected information about various topics. Modern science was born and the Royal Society has continued its work to the present day.

William Harvey (1578–1657).

The founder of modern medicine

Like many other young doctors, Harvey studied at the University of Padua, in Italy. He became a successful London physician but privately carried out innumerable dissections of birds, animals and human beings, until he had built up a practical knowledge of anatomy.

This led directly to his discovery of how blood circulates in the human body, but publication of the discovery in 1616 aroused such furious enmity that for a time he believed himself ruined. His discovery transformed medicine and surgery.

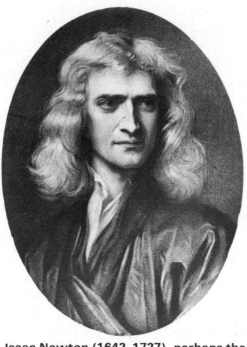

Isaac Newton (1642–1727), perhaps the world's greatest scientific genius.

A scientific genius

While Newton was studying at Cambridge, plague closed the university, so the student went home and, at the age of twenty-three, made three discoveries which revolutionised human thought.

The fall of an apple led him to discover the laws of gravity; his interest in light enabled him to arrive at its composition and to invent a reflecting telescope, and he also introduced the branch of mathematics called calculus.

His book, "Principia", has been called "the greatest single work of science in the world".

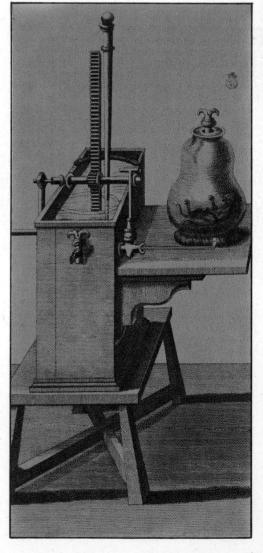

Boyle's air-pump, with an experimental rat. Robert Boyle (1627–91), the founder of modern chemistry, overthrew old ideas about elements and made many discoveries about air, gases, acids and alkalis.

Telescope covered in tooled leather and made in 1661; in the foreground are the covers which would protect the lenses. A telescope of this size would probably have only moderate magnification.

The first telescopes

Roger Bacon, the thirteenth-century friar, is said to have invented a telescope but he probably only realised how one could be made, and the first instrument seems to have appeared in 1608 in Holland, where the Dutch were expert spectacle-makers. The invention consisted of placing two lenses a distance apart in a tube so that distant objects were magnified.

Galileo, hearing of the device, and using a concave lens for the eye-piece, constructed a telescope with which he discovered Jupiter's satellites and the mountains of the Moon. Kepler's telescope used two convex lenses to obtain a bigger field of view.

This engraving shows Fame crowning a bust of Charles II, supported by Francis Bacon and Lord Brounker, President of the Royal Society.

Early members included Robert Boyle, Christopher Wren, Evelyn, Pepys and Doctor Wilkins, Cromwell's brother-in-law, who was the first secretary.

The Royal Society

In the above engraving, you can see some of the crude instruments which members of the Royal Society had to use in their experiments—dividers, set-squares, scales, pendulum, drill, pestles, a gun and, in the field outside, a giant telescope.

One of their great difficulties was in obtaining laboratory apparatus which was sufficiently well-made and accurate, so men like Boyle and Newton had actually to make their own apparatus.

A New Weapon— the Press

The first English newspaper appeared on December 12, 1620, in Amsterdam. It was a single sheet, the first of the *Corantos*, meaning "foreign newspapers". These *Corantos* became sufficiently popular to be published in England, where they were eventually banned.

From 1641, however, Samuel Pecke's "news-books" reported Parliamentary debates and, during the Civil War, Fleet Street kept up an amazing output of news-sheets. Pym, in particular, realised that the printed word was a powerful weapon, and the Royalists reckoned that their own weekly, *Mercurius Aulicus*, was worth a regiment of cavalry.

With the war over, censorship became stricter; Cromwell banned all news-books, except those written by Marchamont Nedham, and the flood of papers which greeted Charles II was soon halted by the Licensing Act, 1662. When the "Gazette", founded in 1665, became the only permitted newspaper, people turned to handwritten sheets, supplied to subscribers and coffee-houses. Not until 1702 did a daily paper, the "Daily Courant", manage to survive more than a few issues.

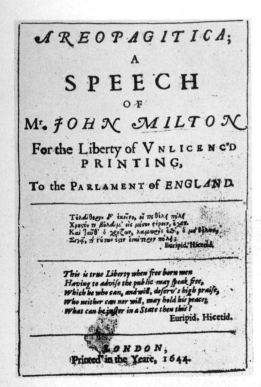

The title-page of *Areopagitica*, John Milton's passionate defence of the freedom of the press, published in 1644. Parliament disappointed him and he placed his hopes on Cromwell, but in vain.

Early journalists

The idea of a free press publishing news of every kind, including criticisms of governments and prominent persons, is still unacceptable in many parts of the world. It is therefore not surprising to find in the sixteenth and seventeenth centuries that journalists led a precarious existence.

Left: "The Man what's got the Whip-hand of them all."—an 18th century cartoon attacking the unbridled freedom of the press to chastise all and sundry.

By the Stamp Act of 1712, the Tories tried to suppress opposition papers by a tax of a half-penny on every half-sheet and a penny on a full sheet. Some papers, like the *Spectator*, paid the tax and survived, others simply increased their size to one and a half sheets and thus escaped the tax.

Freedom of the press

William III, accustomed to a free press in Holland, put an end to censorship and politicians began to hire writers to put their views to the public.

Daniel Defoe was the first professional journalist and he was followed by Addison, Steele and Swift. Steele's prosecution for attacking the government caused a tremendous outcry, and the Tories failed to tax newspapers out of existence.

Jonathan Swift (1667–1745), clergyman, journalist and satirist. By an irony of fate, his greatest work, *Gulliver's Travels*, became a book for children.

An unhappy genius

Swift was born in Ireland and first came to England as secretary to a kinsman. He entered the Church but turned to writing and quickly became celebrated for his wit and biting satire. He described satire as a looking-glass in which people saw every face but their own.

A clergyman in Ireland, Swift constantly visited London, where he became a friend of Addison, Steele and other writers, but joined their political enemies, the Tories, and through his articles in the "Examiner", became so influential that Doctor Johnson said he dictated the political opinions of the English nation. In 1713, he was made Dean of St Patrick's, Dublin, but Queen Anne's hostility put an end to further advancement and he settled into an embittered exile.

Though he loathed Ireland, he championed Irish liberty and, in "Drapier's Letters", brilliantly exposed the injustices which the people suffered. His most widely read book, "Gulliver's Travels", appeared in 1724 but, despite further successes, he fell into increasing unhappiness and despair, until the insanity which he feared overwhelmed him.

Swift spent his life mocking the human race but he was not personally unkind; Addison called him, "the most agreeable companion, the truest friend and the greatest genius of his age."

A fore-runner of *Hansard*, which, since 1774, has printed all debates in the House of Commons. Above is an illustrated page from an early newspaper containing long and graphic accounts of parliamentary business. This had begun in 1641, when Samuel Pecke published a news-book called *A Perfect Diurnal of Occurrences in Parliament*. From this time on, newspapers began to include home affairs, instead of dealing solely with news from abroad.

The Merry Monarch

The traditional picture of Charles II is of the Merry Monarch, the shrewd and witty King who was too indolent to be a capable ruler. In fact, he was remarkably successful, and left the monarchy much stronger than he found it.

Charles admired France and the French way of life, especially the absolute power of the French King, but his own power was severely limited by Parliament's control of his income. By a secret agreement with Louis XIV, Charles obtained sufficient money to make himself to some degree independent, but joining the French against the Dutch Protestant Republic was unpopular and when the Popish Plot provoked an anti-Catholic outburst, Charles had to bow to the storm.

It looked as though Parliament had won and even as if another civil war was brewing. But Charles kept his head. Biding his time, he waited until the hysteria had died down, then suddenly dissolved Parliament and lived out the rest of his life on a comfortable income from France. The King had triumphed, and the Stuart collapse three years later was due to the folly of his brother, James.

A triumphal arch in classical style, designed for the City of London to celebrate Charles II's coronation.

The French game of Pall Mall or *pell mell*, a forerunner of croquet, which the exiled Cavaliers brought back to England.

New architecture

The classical style which Inigo Jones introduced into England became established after the Restoration when architects such as John Webb, Hugh May and Roger Pratt carried on Jones's work.

The Great Fire provided Christopher Wren with the opportunity to prove his genius; he designed fifty-three of the city's churches and his masterpiece, St Paul's Cathedral, as well as Hampton Court Palace, Chelsea and Greenwich Hospitals.

Outdoor amusements

The people's enjoyment of outdoor life is seen in the popularity of the new royal parks, where they could walk about, play games and watch the chariot- and horse-racing. In the Spring Garden by Whitehall and in the New Garden at Vauxhall, they strolled along gravelled walks and refreshed themselves with jellies, tarts, and syllabub (sweet wine and cream).

The King was an enthusiastic sportsman and he was invariably up early to ride with his dogs, to hunt, to sail his yacht or to set out for Newmarket, where he founded horse-racing as a sport.

Pall-mall, fencing, tennis and golf were aristocratic amusements but, in most towns, the bowling-green was the centre for evening entertainment and dancing, and, with the Puritan ban on games lifted, quoits, skittles, football, a kind of cricket, fishing, skating and even bell-ringing became popular pastimes.

The Ball at the Hague (above), a Dutch painting showing Charles dancing with his sister Mary, Princess of Orange.

Left: a cittern (top), an instrument second in importance only to the lute; a 17th century viol (below); groups of bass, tenor and treble viols were very popular.

English music

The sixteenth century saw an unequalled flowering of English music. The "air" or song was brought to perfection by John Dowland and there developed a variety of plucked instruments, including Elizabeth's favourite, the orpharion. These, together with the citterns and lutes, created groups, producing music with richly varied tone colours.

Around 1620, the style changed. One instrument in a group would take over from the rest; the violin, formerly a street instrument, began to oust the viol.

Flutes became very popular, but by the end of the century, the harpsichord and violin had taken precedence over all other instruments.

The connection with Holland

In his tastes and affections, Charles II preferred France to Holland. His mother was French and his favourite sister, "Minette", was married to Louis XIV's brother; France had given him shelter and, after the Restoration, Louis kept him supplied with cash. French manners and the Catholic religion had more appeal for Charles than the earnest Protestantism of Dutch burghers.

These French sympathies were by no means pleasing to the English, who, while they regarded the Dutch as their rivals at sea, sided with them in their life-or-death struggle against Louis XIV. Hence, at one time in the reign, England joined Holland in an alliance against France, but, later, an Anglo-French fleet fought a great sea-battle against the Dutch navy.

Candidates for the throne

The position was further complicated by Charles's family connections. His sister, Mary, had married the Dutchman, William of Orange, and their son, also William, married his English cousin, Mary, daughter of James, Duke of York. Since Charles had no legitimate heir, the crown should pass to his brother, James, an avowed Catholic, but, with the English as strongly anti-Catholic as ever, this Protestant couple, William of Orange and Mary, were obvious candidates for the throne. In fact, they became joint-sovereigns in 1688.

The Merchants Grow Richer

By the seventeenth century, English noblemen and merchants readily put up the money to found trading companies and colonies abroad. Companies, such as the Virginia Company, the East India Company, and the African Company were granted sole rights to trade in particular areas, and, in order to out-manoeuvre the Dutch, Parliament passed Navigation Acts, by which goods from Asia, Africa and America were to be carried only in English ships. In theory, England would prosper by trading with her own colonial possessions and by becoming independent of foreign countries.

In practice, things were less simple. The value of sugar from Barbados was much greater than that of the goods bought by the planters; the North American colonies produced little that was wanted in England, except tobacco, and the much-desired goods from the East had to be paid for largely in gold. African slaves, sold to the Spanish in America, produced large profits for the Royal African Company, but, despite all efforts, colonial trade could not compare with England's trade with Europe.

Sugar from Barbados: a cargo being unloaded at Bristol. The island of Barbados was acquired in Charles I's reign and the early settlers had a hard time until, in 1641, sugar-cane growing was introduced from Brazil.

Hazards of trade: sailors row ashore from a shipwreck off the coast of West Africa; they came for ivory, dyes, hides and slaves.

An elephant-battle, staged as an entertainment for Akbar (1556–1603), greatest of the Mogul emperors, who brought all the provinces of northern India under his wise and tolerant rule.

India in turmoil

When the Europeans—the Portuguese, followed by the Dutch and the English—first arrived in India and began to set up "factories" (trading-posts) on the coast-line, northern India was a united Moslem empire. Its rulers, known as the Grand Moguls, presided over a civilisation whose magnificence astounded the foreigners, but a swift decline occurred during the reign of Aurangzeb (1658–1707).

Having provoked the Hindus to rebellion, he embarked on a series of disastrous wars with the Mahrattas. Under their great leader, Shivaji, they became strong enough to challenge the Mogul empire.

As India fell into a state of turmoil, the foreigners, especially the English, took the opportunity to expand their trading and political activities.

Europeans in India

Portugal led the way to India by sea. In 1498, Vasco da Gama reached Calicut and, for a century, Portuguese traders had the East to themselves. They established settlements on the east and west coasts of India and were strongly entrenched when the English and the Dutch arrived soon after 1600.

In a ferocious three-cornered struggle for the Malayan Archipelago, the Dutch drove out the Portuguese and harried the English in the Spice Islands. They massacred English merchants at Amboyna in 1623 and, although Cromwell later obtained compensation, the English were compelled against their will to concentrate on India. Holland was not strong enough to operate both in India and South-East Asia, so, by the Restoration, the English had little to fear from their rivals.

English trading stations

Their first trading-station was established at Surat in 1613 and, on the east coast, at Musilipatam. In 1640, Fort St George was built at Madras, other factories were opened in Bengal and, by 1647, the East India Company possessed twenty-three stations in India.

Charles II gave the Company the port of Bombay, a most valuable acquisition, because the French had now arrived and, for the next century, they were to be deadly rivals for trade and political power.

Map of India in the 17th century, showing the principal posts set up by foreign trading-companies.

Relations were friendly at first, and the Emperor or some local prince would grant a *nishan* (royal order) to trade, on payment of so many rupees a year.

As the Mogul Empire began to break up and lawlessness increased, the foreigners would sometimes seize a town and fortify it to protect their goods, and this would lead to a destruction of settlements as a reprisal.

A fleet operating along the coast proved a boon to the English East India Company, protecting the settlements and earning goodwill by also safeguarding Indian coastal trade.

Life in Restoration England

Restoration England saw a sudden increase in the number of travellers and vehicles on the roads. The war was over, life was safer and people felt the urge to see the country and visit relatives who, quite probably, had fought on the other side.

People like Defoe, Celia Fiennes and John Evelyn made extensive journeys, which, in days of appalling roads and uncomfortable inns, were expeditions that called for courage and a sense of humour. They kept journals of their travels, recording the neat country towns they passed through, the great mansions they visited, spas where they drank the medicinal waters and the dangers of losing the way or of falling into flooded pot-holes. They noted new industries, like stocking-making and glass-blowing, the post-boys who galloped past with Charles II's newly-instituted Royal Mail, the prosperity of the farmers and the dismal poverty of the workers.

Most travellers went on horseback, changing horses at inns, but a variety of vehicles appeared, including stage-coaches, private carriages and the great stage-waggons, lumbering along at two miles an hour.

The poor

A labourer's wage (3d a day, with food and drink) was precisely the same in Wiltshire in 1655 as in 1603. This was probably due to a plentiful supply of workers but, with prices and other wages rising, a labourer, his wife and children could just exist by all of them working from dawn to dusk.

Illness or a bad harvest brought disaster. Help then depended upon the Poor Law, by which church-wardens in every parish acted as overseers of the poor, setting child-ren to work, providing materials such as wool and iron, and occasion-ally building a cottage and paying out small sums. In practice, most authorities avoided raising a regu-lar poor-rate and did as little as possible, unless alarmed by famine or riots.

Private charity was more gener-ous, and most towns had their almshouses and charitable funds left by wealthy men to help the poor.

Bad roads

The country's roads, neglected since Roman times, had become so bad that travel and transport of goods were slow and perilous.

From 1663, toll-gates were erect-ed on main roads, where travellers had to pay a fee, which was sup-posed to be used for road-repairs. Unfortunately, no-one knew much about the technique of road-making and there was little improvement for a century.

Heavy goods were transported as far as possible by water; rivers were deepened to make them navigable.

a Confectioner   a Smith   a Sho=maker   a Taylor

a Sadler   a Porter   a Box-maker   a Sope-boyler

A broadsheet of 1647 shows a selection of London tradesmen.

Industry

Four-fifths of the people still earned their living on the land, but industry was becoming increasingly important. England was now the biggest coal-producer in Europe and iron-smelting and salt-production began to be concentrated in the Midlands.

The woollen cloth industry was increasingly controlled by the wealthy clothiers who bought the wool and distributed it to spinners; they collected the yarn for the weavers and passed on the cloth to various "finishers" and dyers. This was the "putting-out" system.

Owing to transport difficulties and costs, local craftsmen supplied every country town with all its needs, except luxuries.

A carter bringing a bale of cloth into town (above, left), and a porter (above), essential workers in towns with narrow streets and alleys. A two-wheel cart could manoeuvre better than huge waggons which, because of the roads, were forbidden to carry more than a ton or to use more than 5 horses.

A housewife returning from market (right); she wears *pattens*, overshoes with raised soles to keep her out of the filth in the streets. Servants did the shopping for well-to-do households; Pepys, for instance, kept two maids, a manservant and a boy.

Above: two methods of transport in the 17th century—on horseback and by horse-drawn coach.

Ladies often rode pillion, seated on a special side-saddle, behind a servant. "Improved" coaches were introduced from France; the body was suspended on leather straps attached to pillars on the axles, a device that reduced bumping on bad roads.

Public stage-coaches now made regular advertised journeys, covering 40 to 50 miles a day, at a cost of a shilling every 5 miles.

The Glorious Revolution

Charles II's brother, James, came to the throne in 1685 as James II. He had a docile Parliament and an assured income, yet, in less than four years, by accident or folly, James was a fugitive and the throne was jointly occupied by his daughter and her Dutch husband. How did this happen?

Certainly, there was no spontaneous uprising of the English people, for the nation which had been so deeply divided over Charles I was strangely indifferent to his son's overthrow. James was a Roman Catholic who had promised to keep his personal religion to himself, but the ease with which he crushed an attempt to put Charles II's illegitimate Protestant son, the Duke of Monmouth, on the throne, led him to believe he could bring back the old religion.

He increased the army, put Catholics in high places, arrested the bishops who opposed his policy and so antagonised everyone that a handful of nobles invited William of Orange to come across and save the Protestant faith. William arrived and James, a veteran soldier and admiral, totally lost his nerve and that, most ingloriously, was "The Glorious Revolution".

James II's feeble act of defiance: escaping down the Thames in a rowboat, he threw the Great Seal, needed for all official documents, into the river.

The throne lost

On the night when Londoners lit bonfires to celebrate the acquittal of the Seven Bishops, seven other lords signed a letter inviting William of Orange to England.

He dared to come only because Louis XIV had moved his armies into the Rhineland; by another lucky chance, the wind blew William clear of a fleet in the Channel and he landed unopposed at Torbay.

James came to meet him but when his best general, Lord John Churchill, deserted him, he returned to London. Here, he learned that his daughter, Anne, had also forsaken him and, in despair, he fled to France.

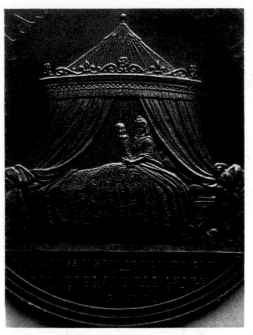

The Catholic heir: James II's wife, Mary of Modena, with her son James. This picture appeared on a coin struck to commemorate the birth.

Louis XIV, in a coat embroidered with captured towns.

Fear of a Catholic King

There were many reasons for the opposition to James II's plan to bring in religious toleration.

The Church of England had been restored as the national Church and the bishops were determined to keep their authority; the Whigs (Parliamentary Opposition) were strongly Protestant and the Puritans and Dissenters regarded Roman Catholics with horror. They believed that James's real intention was to crush Protestantism, as Louis XIV had done in France.

At his accession, James promised to maintain the Church of England; his daughters, Mary and Anne, had been brought up as Protestants and, by his second wife, Mary of Modena, he had no children. Hence, the birth of her son in 1688 was regarded as a catastrophe, for a Catholic line of kings now seemed certain.

Rumours went about that the Queen had not given birth, but that a baby had been introduced into the palace in a warming-pan. True or false, the country now had a Catholic heir to the throne.

The joint monarchs

Mary was James II's daughter by his first wife, Anne Hyde. Brought up as a Protestant, she was married in 1677 to her cousin, William of Orange who, from his defence of Holland, was regarded as a Protestant hero; his possible accession to the throne (he was Charles II's nephew) was talked about by those who feared the King's Catholic leanings.

But, in 1688, what was William's position to be? He soon let it be known he had no intention of becoming his wife's subject. Without more ado, Parliament agreed that he and Mary should be joint sovereigns.

A Delft-ware plate of 1690, portraying the new Protestant sovereigns, William and Mary. After Mary's death, he reigned as William III.

Popery's Downfall and the Protestant's Uprising—cover of a printed copy of a popular song sung by triumphant Protestants in 1688.

The Settlement

Having agreed that James II had abdicated, Parliament let William and Mary know the terms on which they should wear their crowns. By the Declaration of Rights, the monarch was to be a Protestant; he must not set aside the laws, as James had done, or raise taxes, or keep an army without Parliament's consent.

When William and Mary agreed to these conditions, the long struggle between Crown and Parliament was ended; the theory of Divine Right was dead and the reign of Parliament seemed to have begun. In fact, William ruled as he thought fit and kept full control of foreign policy, but he was never an absolute monarch, for he ruled within the law and with Parliament's assent.

The letter, signed by seven lords, which invited William to England.

British Isles and Ireland

This period of religious conflict, of civil war between King and Parliament and of hostilities against Spain, Holland and France includes some of the greatest names in literature, science and the arts—Shakespeare, Milton, Newton, Boyle, Harvey, Wren and Purcell.

Europe

Overseas possessions gave Spain a century of power; Holland and Sweden prospered; religious wars distracted France and Germany; Louis XIV emerged. Renaissance spread across Europe.

1485

Henry VII established Tudor Dynasty; abolished private armies; invaded France, bought off by Charles VIII.
Statute of Drogheda (Poyning's Law); Irish parliament made subordinate to English parliament.
Perkin Warbeck attempted to gain throne; executed. John Cabot reached Newfoundland and N. American mainland (*1497*).
Accession of Henry VIII (*1509*); m. Catherine of Aragon.
Scots defeated at Flodden (*1513*). Field of the Cloth of Gold (*1520*).
Divorce Question brought about Wolsey's fall; Act of Supremacy (*1534*).
Dissolution of Monasteries; Pilgrimage of Grace; executions of Anne Boleyn and Thomas More.
Ireland made a kingdom (*1542*).
Scots defeated at Solway Moss, made alliance with France.
Coverdale's English Bible. Holbein's paintings. Hampton Court built.
Debasement of coinage.
Accession of Edward VI (*1547*). Cranmer's Prayer-Book.

Spain ended Moorish power and conquered an empire in the New World. Portugal's brief period of greatness.
In Germany and Switzerland, Luther, Calvin, and Zwingli attacked the Papacy and ushered in the Reformation.
Peasants' War in Germany ruthlessly suppressed.
Council of Trent (*1545*), beginning of the Counter-Reformation.
Rise of the Habsburgs in Bohemia. Scandinavia adopted Protestant religion.
Florence ruled by the Medici family: period of the Borgias and corrupt Popes.
Intellectual and artistic supremacy of Italy (Michelangelo, Leonardo, Raphael, Titian etc.)
Renaissance culture spread into western Europe.
Copernicus published discoveries in astronomy.

1550

Mary's accession (*1553*); Wyatt's rebellion, execution of Lady Jane Grey.
Marriage of Mary and Philip II of Spain—Catholic religion restored, persecution of Protestants.
War with France, loss of Calais.
Elizabeth's accession (*1558*); Church of England established.
John Knox in Scotland; Mary, Queen of Scots, deposed; executed (*1587*).
Hostility to Spain, assistance to Netherlands. Drake sailed round the world.
Spanish Armada destroyed (*1588*). Cadiz stormed (*1597*).
Irish rebellion led by O'Neill, Earl of Tyrone, subdued by Mountjoy.
Rebellion and execution of Earl of Essex.
Charter of East India Company (*1600*).
William Cecil, Lord Burleigh, was Elizabeth's chief minister.
Renaissance architecture appeared in England; golden age of music—Campion, Byrd, Tallis.
Spenser, Sidney, Wyatt, Donne writing poetry. First theatres built; Kyd, Ben Jonson, Marlowe and Shakespeare wrote plays.

Religious wars in France; Massacre of St Bartholomew (*1572*).
Edict of Nantes (*1598*) gave some relief to Huguenots.
Spain entered golden age in art, music, literature; gained control of southern Italy, failed to conquer Netherlands and England.
Pope Gregory XIII reformed the calendar.
In Russia, Ivan the Terrible gave trading rights to England.
Turkish sea-power broken by Spain and Venice at Battle of Lepanto (*1571*).
Danish astronomer, Brahe, made discoveries.
Gerhard Mercator devised chart for navigators.
Rapid decline of Italian city-states: Milan, Venice, Florence and Genoa lost importance and became dominated by foreign powers.

1600

The Poor Law (*1601*) required each parish to care for the needy.
Accession of James VI of Scotland to English throne as James I (*1603*).
Gunpowder Plot (*1605*); penal laws against Catholics and Puritans.
Plantation of Ulster by English and Scottish settlers.
Authorised Bible published.
Growing tension between King and Parliament.
Accession of Charles I (*1625*). Buckingham's disastrous conduct of affairs.
Petition of Right (*1628*) expressed Parliament's anger at royal absolutism.
Rule without Parliament (*1629–40*); the Bishop's War; arrest of Archbishop Laud; execution of Strafford. Massacre of Protestants in Ireland.
Outbreak of Civil War (*1642*), rise of Cromwell, his decisive victories at Marston Moor, Naseby.
Execution of Charles I (*1649*). The Commonwealth.
Inigo Jones introduced classical architecture into England.
Shakespeare's greatest plays produced.
William Harvey discovered the circulation of the blood.
John Milton writing poetry and republican pamphlets.

Spain: sharp decline of trade and industry; Church all-powerful, merchants and others emigrated. Cervantes wrote Don Quixote (*1605*).
France, under Richelieu's leadership, became stronger than Spain.
Germany: a revolt in Bohemia developed into the Thirty Years' War (*1618–48*), a European struggle between Catholics and Protestants. France and Sweden invaded Germany.
Sweden became strongest Baltic power.
Golden Age of Netherlands: art and music flourished; Holland the commercial centre of Europe, with riches from its newly-acquired empire. Venice fell into decline.
Dutch lens-grinders made first refracting telescope and compound microscope (*c. 1600*).
Kepler established laws of planetary motion.

1650

Republican government; Cromwell massacred Irish at Drogheda and Wexford, defeated Scots at Dunbar, Charles II at Worcester (*1651*).
Cromwell became Lord Protector. Puritan rule in England.
War with Holland and Spain; Admiral Blake's victories; Jamaica captured.
Restoration of Charles II (*1660*); revival of theatre and music; French cultural influence.
Great Plague, Fire of London. Dutch in the Medway. Secret Treaty of Dover (*1670*).
Clarendon Code imposed penalties on Catholics and Dissenters. Covenanters persecuted in Scotland.
The Popish Plot—anti-Catholic riots.
Rye House Plot (*1683*).
James II (*1685–8*) defeated Monmouth's rebellion; tried to restore Catholic religion. Forced into exile.
William and Mary became joint sovereigns.
Writers—Milton, Bunyan, Herrick, Dryden, Congreve, Pepys, Evelyn.
Architect—Christopher Wren; Musician—Henry Purcell.

1689

Scientists—Newton, Boyle, Hooke.

Louis XIV, absolute ruler of France, seized Spanish Netherlands, crushed Huguenots, made France the arbiter of elegance and taste.
Great age of French drama—Corneille, Racine, Molière.
Wars between Holland and England, but a Dutchman became King of England.
Amsterdam the business centre of the world.
Sweden dominated the Baltic area. Swiss cantons at war with one another.
Flowering of Italian opera (Monteverdi, Scarlatti).
Period of Baroque art and architecture.
Huygens invented pendulum clock; Liebritz developed calculus at same time as Newton.
New foods and crops entered Europe, e.g. potato, maize, tea, chocolate, tobacco, coffee, sugar-cane, cotton.

Asia

Break-up of Mogul Empire gave Europeans opportunities to penetrate India, but China and Japan virtually closed to foreigners. Russia began to arise and to check the Ottoman Turks.

Ashikaga period in Japan; collapse of feudal system; civil war and military dictatorship. Jesuit missionaries introduced Christianity. Japanese pirates besieged Nanking.
Ottoman Turks made conquests; penetrated eastern Europe, captured Belgrade, invaded Persia and reached N.W. India.
Ivan the Terrible assumed title of Czar, extended his rule across Siberia.
Portuguese established trading-posts in India; acquired Goa, captured Malacca, became first Europeans to land in Japan.
Babar founded Mogul Empire in India.

Akbar the Great ruled Mogul Empire, a wise and tolerant ruler, presiding over a magnificent civilisation.
English, Dutch, French traders active in the Levant (Near East); Dutch reached Spice Islands.
Ivan the Terrible conquered Siberia. Russian Church became independent of the West.
Portuguese settlement at Macao, off China's coast.
Japanese invaded Korea; their pirates active through Far Eastern waters. Japanese population divided by law into 4 classes—warriors, farmers, merchants, artisans.

Romanov dynasty established in Russia.
Persia ruled by Shah Abbas I, the Great, defeated the Ottoman Turks.
English East India Company obtained trading rights in India, granted sites at Surat and Madras.
Dutch ousted Portuguese from Spice Islands, massacred English merchants at Amboyna.
Bubonic plague in India. Taj Mahal built by Shah Juhan.
China; last Ming Emperor committed suicide (1644), succeeded by Ch'ing or Manchu dynasty. Korea brought under Manchu rule. Japanese capital established at Edo (Tokyo). Tokugawa period—isolation from rest of the world, suppression of Christianity, flowering of national arts.

Dutch took Sumatra from Portuguese.
Ottoman Turks invaded Europe and fought against Austria, Russia, Poland and Venice.
India: reign of Aurangzeb—persecution of Hindus and wars against the Mahrattas of Deccan weakened the Mogul Empire.
Rise of the Sikhs as a powerful military group.
English ousted the Portuguese, acquired Bombay; Anglo-French rivalry commenced.
K'ang Hsi, first of the great Manchu emperors, ruled for more than 50 years, expanded empire, captured Formosa, defeated Mongols, favoured Christian missionaries and brought peace to his dominions.

Africa

While N. Africa fell into the hands of the Moslem Turks who penetrated the Sahara and destroyed native cultures, Europeans made settlements along the coasts and began the slave trade.

Spanish campaigns in North Africa forced Moslem rulers to pay tribute.
Egypt conquered by the Turks.
Portuguese trading along the west coast, penetrated Congo, converted king of Congo Empire; founded Mozambique and ascended Zambezi.
Songhoy Empire under Askia Mohammed conquered Mandingo Empire, but defeated by Haussa Confederation which became dominant power east of the Niger.
Mission of Francisco Alvarez to Ethiopia.
Spanish captured Tunis from the Turks.

Portuguese missionaries in Ethiopia; their success resulted, however, in their eventual expulsion.
British began slave trade from W. Africa to New World.
Empire of Kanem or Bornu supreme in Lake Chad area.

Portuguese settled in Angola but defeated in Morocco.
Turks regained Tunis; penetrated Songhoy Empire, established themselves at Timbuktu and destroyed Negro culture.
Dutch established themselves on Guinea coast and also took Mauritius.
Portuguese explorers penetrated interior from upper Zambezi.
French established a post on the Senegal, settled in Madagascar.
Dutch challenged Portuguese on Gold Coast and built forts.

Capetown founded by the Dutch.
Rise of Bambara Kingdoms on upper Niger.
England acquired Tangier from Portugal, but abandoned it to Sultan of Morocco.
Royal African Company founded for slave-dealing.
French captured Dutch posts on Senegal, attacked Algiers pirates and rescued Christian slaves.

The Americas

While Spain won an empire, destroying the Aztec and Inca civilisations, other Europeans challenged her monopoly of the New World. The English colonised N. America's eastern seaboard.

Columbus sailed to West Indies and claimed all territories for Spain (1492).
John Cabot reached Newfoundland and N. American continent (1497).
Amerigo Vespucci reached S. America (1499); the Portuguese landed in Brazil (1500). Balboa discovered Pacific Ocean (1513).
Magellan circumnavigated the world; Cortez conquered Aztec Empire of Mexico (1518–22); Pizarro destroyed Inca Empire in Peru (1533). Maya Indians conquered. Spanish settlements established in West Indies and on mainland; Negro slavery introduced.
Jacques Cartier explored Gulf of St Lawrence and French made unsuccessful attempt to colonise St Lawrence valley.

French, English and Dutch attacks on Spanish monopoly in the New World. Drake extended raids to the Pacific, claimed California for England.
Spanish Inquisition introduced in Mexico and Peru; native Indians enslaved.
Gilbert claimed Newfoundland for Queen Elizabeth.
English failed to found colony of Virginia in 1584 and 1587.
French attempt to found a colony in Florida overthrown by Spanish; de Champlain explored St Lawrence.

English colony of Virginia founded (1607); tobacco cultivated.
Henry Hudson explored Hudson River.
French founded Quebec (1608).
Dutch fur-traders on Manhattan Island (1613); founded New Amsterdam.
Pilgrim Fathers settled at Plymouth, Massachusetts (1620).
English settlers arrived at Salem (1628) and 400 Puritans, led by John Winthrop, reached Massachusetts Bay (1629).
Harvard College founded (1636).
Swedish settlement at Fort Christina.
Spanish power declined and English, French and Dutch obtained footing in West Indies. Catholic Church acquired vast wealth and influence in S. America.

British captured Jamaica; seized New Amsterdam from Dutch and renamed it New York (1664).
Spanish Jesuits established missions in Arizona and California.
English Quakers settled in New Jersey (1676) and, led by William Penn, in Pennsylvania (1681).
Spanish commerce declined under attacks by English, French and Dutch pirates.
Carolina granted to eight proprietors by Charles II.
Dutch expelled from Brazil by Portuguese.
La Salle reached mouth of Mississippi and claimed whole valley for France.

Europe

ATLANTIC OCEAN

SCOTLAND

IRELAND

WALES

ENGLAND

NORTH SEA

ENGLISH CHANNEL

Holland

Spanish
Netherlands

FRANCE

Aragon

SPAIN

NORWAY

SWEDEN

BALTIC
SEA

DENMARK

ESTHONIA

LIVONIA

KURLAND

RUSS

PRUSSIA

POLAND

HOLY ROMAN EMPIRE

Bohemia

HUNGARY

PAPAL STATES

OTTOMAN EMPIRE

NAPLES

MEDITERRANEAN SEA

① ② ③ ④ ⑤ ⑥ ⑦ ⑧ ⑨ ⑩ ⑪ ⑫ ⑬ ⑭